GATORIN'

TAILS & TALES

GATORIN'
TAILS & TALES

A Legacy of Family, Faith, and
Florida Alligator Trapping

DR. CHARLIE RENTZ

Copyright © 2025 by Dr. Charles D. Rentz.

All rights reserved. No part of this book may be used or reproduced in any form whatsoever without written permission except in the case of brief quotations in critical articles or reviews.

Some of the names in this book have been changed to show respect for the individuals and their stories.

Cover image, design, and interior formatting provided by Casselberry Creative Design.

Story Sanctum Publishing, LLC

ISBN: 979-8-9928559-5-1

GLOSSARY OF TERMS

Gatorin' (ga-tor-in). *Noun*. The art of hunting and capturing an alligator.

Word History: The word gatorin' was used and passed down by my great grandfather, Robert Lawrence Pappy (1870-1945) to describe the activity of hunting and capturing alligators. Robert was a third generation native Floridian, cowboy, cracker, butcher, jelly maker and fourth generation alligator trapper.

Tails (teylz). *Noun*. The hind most parts of animals, especially when prolonged beyond the rest of the body; the flexible extension of the backbone in a vertebrate, such as in an alligator.

Tales (teylz). *Noun*. A word referring to a story or a narrative; describes an imaginative or true event that can be creatively embellished.

The tales contained in this book are true, unembellished stories from actual events told by Charlie Rentz, Licensed Nuisance Alligator Trapper, a sixth generation native Floridian and a seventh generation alligator trapper. You can't begin to make this stuff up. I promise!

To my family who came before me and to my family who will live on after me, I dedicate this book. This is our legacy.

WARNING

Alligator trapping is extremely dangerous and should never be attempted without proper training and authorization. The accounts in this book reflect the personal experiences of a licensed, professional nuisance alligator trapper and are shared for storytelling and entertainment purposes only. If you encounter an alligator, do not approach or attempt to capture it—maintain a safe distance, do not harass and do not feed alligators. Violating alligator laws can result in severe penalties, including felony charges and fines. If you believe you have a nuisance alligator, contact the SNAP Hotline at 1-866-FWC-GATOR (Florida only) or your local wildlife authorities immediately.

Table of Contents

GLOSSARY OF TERMS	5
WARNING	9
INTRODUCTION	13
CHAPTER ONE	15
CHAPTER TWO	25
CHAPTER THREE	43
CHAPTER FOUR	57
CHAPTER FIVE	63
CHAPTER SIX	91
CHAPTER SEVEN	99
CHAPTER EIGHT	105
CHAPTER NINE	111
CHAPTER TEN	121
EPILOGUE	127
PICTURE INDEX	131
ACKNOWLEDGMENTS	139
ABOUT THE AUTHOR	142

INTRODUCTION

People are bound together by their common stories: whether it be through a community, a religion, a club, a sports team, a school, college, university, or a country. These groups of people share common stories. Even a family, or maybe I should say, especially a family, shares common stories that are unique to the members of that particular family.

Take for instance the Bible. The Bible is essentially a book of stories. Many of the stories in the Bible are about love, peace, grace, mercy, forgiveness, faith, and hope. Wonderful stories! But there are also stories about hate, murder, rape, incest, betrayal, lies, deception, war, and evil. God-awful stories! One thing we know is that these stories were shared from generation to generation by what is known as the oral tradition. These stories were shared for thousands of years before they were ever written down. Storytelling is the oldest thing that people do in community. My family has their own unique stories that have been passed down through the ages from generation to generation by our own oral tradition. Many of my family stories involve gatorin'.

At the time of this writing, I am 69 years old and have been a Licensed Nuisance Alligator Trapper for many years. I have personally trapped, captured, handled, and tagged hundreds of alligators. The number is well over one thousand if you also count the captures in which I assisted other trappers. No two captures are ever the same. Each one tests you in new ways, and every time, danger is close enough to taste. One wrong move, one second of distraction, and you could lose a hand, a foot, or even your life. No matter how often I do it, there's always an adrenaline rush.

Catching alligators may seem like a very strange and unusual family tradition. This book is a collection of stories telling my family's history of gatorin'. I will also share many of my own stories of captures, personal encounters, experiences, and interactions with alligators and with the people who were involved in the captures.

I began learning the art of catching and handling alligators over 60 years ago from my maternal grandfather, F. Gerald Pappy. The things he did, what he showed me, and what he said to me when I began accompanying him as an eight-year-old boy still echo in my head with each and every alligator I encounter.

CHAPTER ONE
All in the Family

I received a call and was issued a permit from the office of SNAP (State Nuisance Alligator Program) about a man who, while fishing from his kayak, had an alligator snatch a fish out of his hand. I was about five minutes from the address and immediately responded. What I found when I arrived was not what I expected. A man, whom I estimated to be around 75 years old, was in the pond behind his house sitting in his kayak. His wife was on the bank, trying not to show her fear, and telling him to just sit still. The poor man was ashen like he had just seen a ghost. All the color had vanished from his face. It was for good reason because there in the water, less than ten feet away, was an eight-foot alligator. I immediately called my good friend and alligator trapping buddy Kevin for help, and thankfully he was also nearby.

This man went out fishing every afternoon in his kayak. It was something he had done for years. On this particular day, he caught a decent size bass, which was not an uncommon experience. But as he reached out to release the bass, this alligator literally snagged it out of his hand. Later after the ordeal was over, he explained how he could feel the breath of the alligator when it chomped down on the bass. Fortunately, and by the grace of God, the alligator got all bass and no fingers, hand, or arm. The problem was that after taking the bass, the alligator then followed the man as he paddled back to his house, which was several hundred yards away from where the alligator had taken the bass.

The man called his wife on his cell phone while still sitting in his kayak and told her what had happened. She notified SNAP, who then notified me. Once the man was back on the side of the pond closest to his house, he was afraid to get out of the kayak (because he would have had to step into the water with the alligator looming close by). Thankfully, Kevin arrived quickly, and together we pulled the man and kayak up on the shore. He was able to get safely out of the kayak and away from the alligator. The poor guy was really shook up thinking about what could have happened. Even with all the commotion we made, the alligator hardly moved. He was hoping for another free meal. Once the man was safely away from the alligator, Kevin and I proceeded to snag, catch, and remove the alligator which measured over eight feet long.

In retrospect, the alligator wasn't doing anything wrong. He was just being an alligator. Evidently, he was new to this pond, and the man certainly wasn't intending to feed him. He said that he never imagined he would see an alligator in his pond since he had never seen one there before. Alligator trappers have a saying when people ask us if there might be an alligator in their lake or pond: reach down and put your hand in the water. If your hand is wet, then there is a good possibility that an alligator may be present. This particular story could have had a tragic ending, but thankfully it didn't. This event happened ten or twelve years ago. I often think about this man but never followed up with him. I wonder if he ever fished from his kayak again. My guess would be that he didn't.

This is but one of the many personal alligator stories that I will share in this book. To understand and appreciate how I became an alligator trapper, I have to begin by telling the story of my family history, particularly how it relates to alligator trapping.

I am a rare find because I am a real live, genuine, bona fide native Floridian. For as long as I can remember, I was told of my Minorcan heritage by my grandfather, Pappy. Over and over, he explained that our ancestors had come to America from Minorca, one of Spain's Balearic Islands in the Mediterranean Sea. Many people confuse Minorca (Menorca) with Mejorca (Mallorca). My ancestors came to America in the 1700's as indentured servants, or "white slaves" as Pappy called them.

While working on my doctorate at Boston University, I took a doctoral level class entitled "The Psychodynamics of Marriage and Family," taught by the renowned professor Dr. John Maes. Dr. Maes was a licensed clinical psychologist and Executive Director of the Albert V. Danielson Institute at Boston University. This particular class turned out to be one that would help shape my life and future. A part of the class involved doing a genealogy of your family. I took this class long before online searches like Ancestry.com, Legacy Tree, and 23andMe were available and before you could use a computer to pull up whatever information you would like to know. It involved extensive work searching through old courthouse records, family Bibles, census records, and much library research.

I was able to trace my family's genealogy back nine generations on both my mother and father's sides of the family. I discovered wonderful stories of faith, hope, and love, along with the realization that I had inherited a strong Christian heritage. I also discovered some God-awful stories that were deeply disturbing. For instance, my great-great-great-great grandfather on my father's side of the family was Captain Jessie Carter (1774-1847). He was a commander in the Indian War of 1838, which forced the removal of the Cherokee Nation from their land. Some 17,000 Cherokee people were taken from their homes in the southeastern United States and forced to march to what is now Oklahoma. It became known as the Trail of Tears that resulted in the deaths of thousands of Cherokee people. How could someone in my family's history have been a part of this? Dealing with this newfound information was difficult. I learned that when you dare to reach back into the past, you had better prepare yourself. You are apt to find some alarming history.

Through the research on my own genealogy, I was able to document what I had always been told. I am a sixth-generation native-born Floridian on my mother's

(Pappy's) side of the family. There is documentation that the American alligator was an integral part of my own family's history and heritage dating back to my family's arrival in Florida in the 1760's. I am fortunate to have the book *Gaspar Papi and Ana Pons - Their Lives and Descendants* written by Latrell Pappy Mickler (copyright 2008) as well as the Pappy family genealogy and history work compiled by Gregory C. White. Both Latrell and Gregory are distant cousins on my mother's side of the family. Their research and documentation have been a vital resource for me.

I love James Michener novels, with my favorites being *Caribbean*, *Hawaii*, and *The Source*. Michener uses historical research and looks at the lives of people from a common ancestry from generation to generation. It takes Michener thousands of pages to do this. I will not go "James Michener" on you and write thousands of pages, but I want to give you a brief history to explain the connection with my family ancestry and alligators.

After the Treaty of Paris was signed in 1763, Spanish subjects in Florida were required to change their allegiance to the new British government or leave the country. A majority of the Spanish residents fled to Cuba, which left a void in the population of the new English colonies of Florida. King George III of England offered land grants in an effort to resettle Florida. One such land grant, known as "Mosquitoes," was allotted to a Scottish physician, Dr. Andrew Turnbull. He founded the colony of New Smyrna, which is now known as New Smyrna Beach, Florida. It consisted of over one hundred thousand acres. The general agreement between Turnbull and any new colonist was an indenture of seven years. An indentured servant was basically an immigrant who signed a contract to work for a specific number of years in exchange for passage to America. Food and shelter would be provided. At the end of their seven-year agreement, each new colonist was promised fifty acres of land plus five bonus acres for each child in the family. One thousand four hundred and three people from the island of Minorca took advantage of this opportunity. On March 31, 1768, the Turnbull fleet sailed from Minorca on eight vessels. All landed safely on the east coast of Florida near present-day New Smyrna Beach.

The new colonists had a very rough beginning. Clearing the land, enduring living in palmetto shacks, dealing with swarms of bugs (mosquitoes, no-see-ums), hurricanes, tropical storms, rattlesnakes, and water moccasins were among the hardships. Attacks from local tribes of Native Americans and an overabundance of alligators also presented challenges to the new settlers. The Minorcan colonists suffered from scurvy, and many died of starvation. Their diet consisted mainly of hominy grits, turkey buzzards, and alligators. Alligator meat is an excellent food source, is high in protein, and tasty if prepared correctly. However, I cannot even begin to imagine being so hungry that I would eat a buzzard to keep from starving to death. By 1769, after just a few months in the new colony, malnutrition, malaria, and other illnesses had taken the lives of 177 of the men, women, and children.

One of the colonists who arrived from Minorca was seventeen-year-old Gaspar Papi (1751-1817). Gaspar was born in what is now modern-day Turkey. He was the son of Miguel Papi and Catalina Ayvas. Gaspar would go on to become my great-great-great-great-grandfather on my mother's side of the family.

Over the next several years, the conditions in New Smyrna never really improved. Colonists were forced to live almost naked, and worked from dawn to dusk. They were flogged. Some were put in the stockade as punishment. Others were chained to a steel ball. Some were even beaten to death as they worked out their period of indenture. Nine years passed, and only six hundred of the colonists were still alive. Their promises of a seven-year indenture and land grants never came true.

In March 1777, some of the Minorcan colonists revolted, escaped, and walked seventy miles north to St. Augustine. Another large group escaped in May 1777, claiming their indenture had expired. By June 1777, most of the Minorcan colonists were freed from Dr. Turnbull by the courts.

Gaspar Papi escaped to St. Augustine, where he began a new life as a farmer and a merchant. It was there that he married a younger Minorcan lady by the name of Ana Pons (1762-1835). They married on February 10, 1781, and Ana would go on to become my great-great-great-great-grandmother. Although Gaspar and Ana had come to America as indentured servants, at the time of Gaspar Papi's death in 1817, he was a successful and respected businessman, Native American interpreter and guide, and government contractor. Gaspar owned five houses in St. Augustine. One of the houses still stands today and is known as the Don Toledo/Gasper Papi house. It is believed to be one of the oldest standing houses in America.

With their strong Roman Catholic background and heritage, Gaspar and Ana went on to have nine children. One of Gaspar and Ana's daughters, Josefa, who was born on November 26, 1795, was the first child to be baptized at the font of the Old Cathedral in St. Augustine when it was completed. The Bishop, Agustin Verot, said, "My child, you shall live over 100 years." Josefa died on June 11, 1896, at the age of 100 years, 6 months, and 15 days (Florida Times-Union, June 12, 1895). One of those great stories of faith, hope, and love!

Gaspar and Ana's youngest child, Jose Vitorio Papi (1802-1853), and his wife Rafaela Olivero, who were my great-great-great-grandparents, had ten children. Their second oldest child was Joseph B. Papy. He and his wife, Louisa Henry, became my great-great-grandparents (notice the change from Papi to Papy, to Americanize the name). Joseph and Louisa gave birth to Robert Lawrence Pappy (1870-1945; notice the change where another "p" was added to their last name). Robert and his wife, Maud Ranger, were my great-grandparents. Their youngest child, Fredrick Gerald Pappy (1910-1994), was my grandfather. He was born on July 13, 1910. He married Leona Ebersol (1910-1984), my grandmother, on August 9, 1930. Gerald and Leona had three daughters. Their oldest child was my mother, Dolores, whose name was very common among Minorcans. She was born on July 12, 1931.

My grandfather had heard and memorized the family stories about his ancestors from his father, Robert Pappy. Robert told stories of his father, Joseph B. Papy, and his grandfather, Jose Vitorio Papi, and even his great-grandfather, colonist Gaspar Papi. Robert told the legend of them all being proud alligator trappers. Jose Vitorio, Joseph, and Robert were all butchers by trade. Alligator hunting, or gatorin' as they called it, was never in any way a hobby. It was a way of life.

A vital part of their family business and income was catching, processing, and selling alligator meat as a food staple. Of course, there was also money to be made from the alligator hides. Perhaps the most powerful and favorite story that endured through the generations was that of seventeen-year-old Gaspar Papi being one of the first and few colonists who made it their job to catch, kill, clean, and even cook alligator meat to keep the colonists from starvation. These stories Robert shared with my grandfather, Pappy, were passed down to my mother, Dolores, and then on to me.

A great deal of historical information about Gaspar and Ana Papi and their descendants has been recorded and documented. For instance, the wills of Gaspar are part of public record. However, the alligator stories are, as far as I know, part of my family's own oral tradition. Do I believe these stories that have endured for generations are true accounts? Absolutely! It only makes sense once you know more of my Pappy's story.

CHAPTER TWO
Pappy

My grandfather, F. Gerald Pappy, or Pappy as everyone called him, was, in fact, a native Floridian Cracker. The word "cracker" is derived from the sound made by the cracking of a whip by cowboys to drive cattle. It is a term used to describe the early pioneers and cattle herders, as well as their culture and descendants, of whom I am one.

When he was twelve years old, Pappy went to work on a cattle ranch as a cowboy. On his sixteenth birthday, Pappy ran away from home, which was near Daytona, Florida, where he was born and raised. He rode his horse to Jacksonville, Florida, never looking back. His father, Robert Lawrence Pappy, had recently moved to Jacksonville to leave the butcher business behind and start a jelly business. Pappy eventually took over the family business, which grew to be known as Pappy Products. His specialty was guava jelly and jam. He also made orange marmalade and watermelon rind preserves. The guava jelly was made at a factory that once sat on what is now Arcadia Drive in the San Jose area of Jacksonville.

Next to the factory was the house in which my mother was born. To my knowledge, that house is still standing today. The property was right next door to Oaklawn Cemetery. Generations of the Pappy family are buried just a couple hundred yards from the property and house in Oaklawn Cemetery, where my mother played and learned to ride her bike as a child. Among those who are buried there are Robert and Maud Pappy, Gerald and Leona Pappy, and Charlie and Dolores Pappy Rentz, who are my parents.

World War II broke out when Pappy was thirty-one years old. He tried to enlist but was not able to pass the physical because of a bad back, which was probably the result of cowboy injuries. Pappy wore a back brace every day of his life. He called it his corset. I suppose it was similar to what President John F. Kennedy wore. Pappy's bad back, however, never slowed him down.

The jelly business was a great success, and my grandparents did well financially. When I was a small child, they sold everything in Jacksonville and bought a fifty-eight-acre farm and a beautiful old farmhouse near Melrose, Florida. It was here they raised Angus cattle, horses, and hogs and continued to make guava jelly. Pappy always had a huge garden.

I loved Pappy and my grandmother, whom I called Nanny. Growing up I spent every moment that I could with them on the farm. Pappy taught me so much about life. I saw cows breed and calves being born. I went to the livestock market where animals were bought and sold. I saw cows and hogs being processed for food. Pappy taught me how to rope and ride and gave me my love for horses. In my mind, as you could say in today's language, I identified as a cracker. I went to work on a horse ranch when I was in high school and college. I even had my own horse.

Many years later, when Marcia and I married, we acquired several horses. I thought it would be a good thing for our children to experience horses and learn to take care of them. We mainly did trail riding as a family, and our daughter, Alaina, entered several western show events. She is an excellent rider. Our other children didn't really connect with and enjoy the horses like Alaina and I did.

I had always ridden Western saddles until I experienced my very first English saddle in my early 50's. I learned to jump and even entered some hunter-jumper events. We sold the horses a few years ago when Alaina went off to college, and I got back two hours of my life every day. Horses take a lot of work and are incredibly expensive to own. As an adult, I often wondered how Pappy was able to take care of everything on the farm. It was definitely a twelve-hour-a-day, seven-day-a-week job for him.

Pappy had a "type A" personality. He never met a stranger, and he loved to talk. As the old adage goes, "He could talk the back legs off a donkey." He was fun to be around. He had a sharp wit, and he loved to joke, tease, and laugh. He had numerous expressions that I call "pappyisms." When my grandmother would get to talking and he wanted to interrupt, he would say, "Excuse me lady, I thought you was the mule." I never really understood what that meant.

My grandmother was a big-boned woman. Her father was a boat builder and a river boat captain in Jacksonville. I remember great-grandpa Ebersol from when I was a child. At eighty years old he still looked like he could play middle linebacker for the Pittsburgh Steelers. Pappy's build, on the other hand, was akin to Barney Fife from *The Andy Griffith Show*. He often said, "I am so glad I married your grandmother. She can keep me warm in the winter and in the summer, I can stand in the shade." As an adult I have often wondered if those words ever really hurt her. If so, she never showed it. She would just laugh it off and say, "Oh Gerald..." Another "pappyism" was him introducing himself by saying, "I have a Mamie and a Pappy and a Grand Mamie Pappy all for a wife."

Pappy always wore Pay Day overalls Monday through Saturday. On Sunday he wore his "go to meetin' clothes," which included a shirt, dress pants, coat, and a tie. He would keep these clothes on all day. He never missed church. He was a trustee, mowed the church lawn on Saturday afternoons, rang the church bell, and ushered on Sunday mornings. My grandmother sang in the choir in their little country Methodist church, and at the time of her death had taught Sunday School for over fifty consecutive years. Nanny was the biggest spiritual inspiration for my life.

Most everyone knew Gerald Pappy as someone who was always smiling, happy, and having fun. However, Pappy had two distinct personalities. Pappy was not only a businessman, but also a wildlife trapper. When he was trapping, he was stern, focused, serious, and extremely cautious. There wasn't a creature he could not or would not catch. He always captured everything alive. Bobcats were one type of animal he trapped. When I was around ten years old, I was with him when he captured the largest bobcat on record in Florida. I remember it being on display at the Greater Jacksonville Fair. I think he still holds the record to this day. He also trapped black bears that got a little too close to civilization. Foxes, coyotes, raccoons, opossums, armadillos, and anything else you can think of were fair game to him. He would dispatch critters like coyotes, raccoons, and others who were a nuisance and caused trouble, like getting into chicken coops. He treated every animal with dignity, especially the ones he had to kill. He reminded us that they were, after all, God's creatures. He had no patience with anyone who would abuse an animal. One of his memorable "pappyisms" was: "Anyone who would abuse any animal would abuse a human being."

    Pappy was the guy to call if you needed something trapped. When I was around ten years old, he built me a couple of box traps, and I caught my own share of critters growing up. Pappy had quite the reputation as a trapper, both when he lived in Jacksonville and later in Melrose. He was especially well known for catching snakes and alligators. The majority of his snake calls came after he moved to Melrose. He caught rattlesnakes and cottonmouth moccasins and sold them to Ross Allen (1908-1981), the famous herpetologist who was based at the Ross Allen Reptile Institute in Silver Springs for forty-six years. Their venom was used to make antivenom. And yes, as a kid, I was taught by him how to catch and handle rattlesnakes.

Neighbors would call whenever one showed up in their barn or horse stalls.

I can remember Pappy taking a plastic tube, putting just a drop or two of gasoline into it, and blowing it into a gopher hole. Often a rattlesnake would emerge, having had his home invaded with the smell of gasoline. It would make the snake madder than an old wet hen. Pappy would use a hook or a sliding noose to catch poisonous snakes. When I got into my teenage years, I would pin the head of a rattlesnake or moccasin with a four-foot-long forked stick that I fashioned and pick it up with my bare hands. I learned how to make the snake open its mouth and reveal its fangs. I *never* let Pappy or my parents know I was handling poisonous snakes with my bare hands. I would still be grounded if they had ever found out! It was much later that I learned that even the world's biggest rattlesnake expert, Ross Allen, had been bitten several times while milking rattlesnakes.

My mother and grandmother would get angry with Pappy for taking me with him when he was catching rattlesnakes. They both hated snakes. Pappy kept the rattlesnakes and moccasins in a cage in an old concrete block carport thirty yards away from the farmhouse. When he had collected enough snakes, he would make a run to Silver Springs which, at the time, was Florida's biggest tourist attraction located in Ocala. Pappy would often joke that if there was an S&H green stamp in the rattlesnake cage, my grandmother would reach in and grab the rattlesnake by the throat just to get the green stamp. Going to the S&H green stamp redemption store with my mother and grandmother is an experience that I would just like to forget. Back in the day, grocery stories gave out green stamps. The more you spent, the more stamps you'd get and could redeem for various items (like token tickets at Chuck E. Cheese). It was boring because they never got anything we liked, just crock pots and toasters. We would rather be at the farm with Pappy, but it seemed that my mother and grandmother lived for green stamps.

I caught non-poisonous snakes for years. They included yellow rat snakes, corn snakes, and hognose snakes which are also called spreading adders. Pappy hooked me up with a guy who bought them for a dollar a foot. He was a middleman who would pick up my captures from Pappy and in turn sell them to pet stores. One quick snake story before we get to the alligator stories: I was around fourteen years old and had caught a croaker sack full of non-poisonous snakes to take to Pappy. I put the sack of snakes in our 1969 Kingswood Estate station wagon, and we headed out from our home in the outskirts of Jacksonville, Florida to Melrose, which was sixty miles away.

It was Mother's Day, and we were going to take Nanny and Pappy to dinner after church. When we arrived in Melrose, I took the sack of snakes to the carport and noticed that one of the snakes was missing. This meant that a four-foot-long yellow rat snake was loose in the car. Being fourteen and having a healthy fear of my parents and grandparents, I failed to mention to them that there was a snake loose in the car. I prayed all the way to Gainesville and back to Melrose that the snake would not reveal itself. Once we returned to Melrose mid-afternoon, I searched everywhere in the car and left the doors open, hoping that it would crawl out. No such luck. That evening as we prepared to make the drive home, with Nanny and Pappy standing outside the car telling us to have safe travels home, the rat snake emerged from under the front passenger seat where my mother was sitting. My mother began to scream and so did Nanny. I came from the back seat to grab the escaping snake that had coiled around my mother's leg. Having to confess that I knew the snake was loose in the car was the worst. My dad wasn't afraid of snakes, but he didn't like them. I am pretty sure that Pappy grinned at me while I was getting lectured. Everyone was in full agreement that if that snake had emerged when we were going sixty miles an hour down the highway, we would have all been killed in a car accident. I think I was grounded for at least a year. That day was the end of my snake-catching career.

  Pappy loved God and lived out his Christian faith. He read a chapter from the Bible every day of his life. He loved my grandmother, whom he affectionately called Old Lady, and teased her every minute they were together. He loved his daughters, and especially his grandchildren. He loved Nellie, his beautiful Palomino quarter horse. He could shoot a shotgun off Nellie while mounted. When I was in high school, I remember Pappy falling off Nellie and breaking his collarbone. On this particular occasion, Nellie stepped into some very soft mud crossing a stream while Pappy was deer hunting. He went head over heels off her. Pappy continued to hunt all day even with a broken collarbone. He was tough!

I believe that Pappy's two biggest passions in life were turkey hunting and telling stories. Anytime he told gatorin' stories, he would become intense as well as animated. It always seemed as if he was sharing the most vital piece of information you would ever receive. It was like he was giving you a detailed map to a buried chest full of gold. One of the stories he must have told a hundred times was about collecting hatchlings with his father, Robert. We would beg him to tell us this story. If it was true, Robert had to be one crazy dude!

Robert would scout out nests where the female gators would lay their eggs. The nests are constructed by the female out of a mound of mud and decomposing vegetation. The nests are built on dry ground very near the water, swamps, or marshes. Nests are usually a couple of feet high and six feet wide. A seasoned alligator trapper can spot one in a second while most people would never notice it. Female gators lay as many as forty to fifty eggs and fiercely guard the nest. Once the eggs hatch, the mama gator will protect her young from predators like raccoons, swamp birds, and especially the papa gator, who will often return to eat the babies. I have caught many females with battle scars like missing limbs, bite marks, and bob tails from defending their nests and young. Mama gator will usually protect the young until the time comes to build a new nest and lay another clutch of eggs. There are few creatures as protective as mama alligators. I will share some of my personal stories about nesting mama gators in a later chapter.

According to Pappy, Robert would never kill a

female alligator. He wanted to come back each year to collect the young hatchlings. Alligators tend to nest in the same place or at least in the close vicinity year after year. Pappy began accompanying Robert on these hunts when he was around eight years old. Pappy was told to stay in a safe place until Robert caught the mama gator, securing her with a noose and rope to a nearby tree or some type of structure, like a piece of pipe driven into the ground. This was done before sunset. Once it got dark, Robert and Pappy used antique flashlights or even torches to locate the hatchlings. They picked them up barehanded and placed them in old pillowcases.

"Would they bite?" we would always ask.

"Sometimes, but it doesn't really hurt. You just need to remember to pick them up by their tails," was always the answer.

According to Pappy, during one night hunt when he was very young, he accidentally dropped his pillowcase somewhere in the swamp. When they got to the nest, there was nothing to put the hatchlings in. So, Robert made Pappy tuck his shirttail in, collected the hatchlings, and put them inside Pappy's shirt against his skin. Pappy would tell us he had fifty baby gators against his bosom.

"Did they bite you?" we always asked.

"Nope, but I had to learn to not be ticklish very quickly," he answered.

"Were you ever afraid?" we asked.

"Lots of times, but I did what my daddy told me to do. I was more afraid of my father than any alligator," he answered.

My questions now would be: how did you know that the mama gator would not get loose and come after you? How would you defend yourself if she got loose while you were stealing her babies? Evidently, no mama ever got loose. I can't even imagine how scary it was for Robert to go back at first daylight to release the mama gator. Robert had to be badder and tougher than Leroy Brown, King Kong, and a junkyard dog.

The sad part of this story is that Robert collected these hatchlings in order to make money to help feed his family. The hatchling alligators were sold as pets to northerners who came to Florida on vacation. Alligators were *never* meant to be kept as pets. Any native Floridian knows that!

Having listened to Pappy's stories for years, I can clearly remember the day when Pappy said, "Boy, it's about time you learned gatorin'." I was eight years old, and we were at our lake house near Seville on Lake George in Volusia County when Pappy took me on a path at night through the swamp to the big lake. We shined up quite a few red eyes. Pappy explained that the redder the eyes, the younger the gator. White eyes were a sign of a very old gator who had cataracts.

We then stood on the bank as Pappy began to grunt up the gators. Within seconds we had several two-foot gators at our feet. He showed me how to slip a noose around the neck of the inquisitive gator, and snug it up, and then keep it away from you when you brought it ashore. He and I caught and released several young ones. We took a two-foot gator up to the back porch of the house. I can't remember if Pappy taped or tied his mouth, but I got to hold him after he did.

The gator wasn't too happy to be caught. It rolled and hissed and called for his mama. He soon calmed down, though, and Pappy taught me how to put him to "sleep" by laying him on his back and stroking his belly from head to tail. They "wake up" when stroked in the opposite direction, like I saw the alligator wrestlers do at the alligator farm in St. Augustine. They really don't go to sleep. It is called tonic immobility. It has to do with the inner ear not receiving the correct signals for orientation, which causes the alligator to appear to temporarily go to "sleep."

I was hooked that night when Pappy began to teach me the correct way to catch and handle alligators. Of course I was—gatorin' was a family tradition! While it must have been fun for Pappy to begin passing on this tradition to yet another generation, he was perfectly clear just how dangerous gatorin' can be. He taught me with his Alligator Pappyisms.

Pappyisms 101: "One wrong move, one stupid decision and you can lose a hand or a foot or an arm or a leg. This is dangerous and you can even lose your life. Never, ever, ever let your guard down. What you see people doing at the alligator farm ain't the real world. Don't ever think you can wrestle a wild alligator or a tame one either because there is no such thing. If the alligator is on land, never walk up on him directly from behind. He can turn and spin around and grab you before you can get out of the way. Don't ever approach him directly from the front because he can charge you. Approach him from the front side on a forty-five-degree angle. An alligator, just like a horse, knows if you don't know what you are doing. Stay calm and move slowly when catching an alligator. Move quickly to stay away from him once he is caught. Be careful and don't take your eyes off his mouth and tail, especially once he has been caught. An alligator's tail is almost as dangerous as his mouth. He can break your leg with a swat of that tail. That tail can easily knock a grown man down. If he knocks you down, you are his. Don't ever wade out in the water to catch an alligator. If you get a gator that is too big for you to handle alone, then leave it alone. There ain't no shame in asking somebody to help you. Gatorin' is safer if you take somebody with you." Each and every time we ever talked gatorin', Pappy would repeat these "Pappyisms" to me over and over and over again for years to come. It was as if he had some foreknowledge of what I would be doing in the future.

I mentioned that Pappy started teaching me when I was eight years old. I literally caught my first alligator at age eight. Unbeknownst to me at that time, eight was the age for the rite of passage to gatorin'. Pappy was eight when his father began to teach him. Pappy also taught my mother beginning when she was around eight years old. Later, as a teenage girl, she would often accompany him when he was catching gators. As my brother and I grew up, we would beg our mother to catch an alligator. She would usually oblige, and she was darn good at it. Because Pappy didn't have any sons, he made sure the family legacy continued with my mother and didn't miss a generation.

I have one very vivid memory from my childhood involving my mother and an over-friendly alligator. My mother, my brother, and I were at our lake house. My dad had to work and would come down on the weekends. There was a four-foot gator that showed up who had no fear of people. Mom told us to leave him alone so he would leave us alone. There were strict rules to never ever, under any circumstances, feed the alligators. This particular gator must have at some point been fed by someone. Perhaps by someone who was fishing nearby. Once an alligator is fed, it begins to lose all fear of humans and simply associates humans with food.

My brother and I were deeply intrigued with this particular gator because he had no fear of us, and we were too stupid to be afraid of him. And maybe (I really don't remember) my brother and I just *might* have thrown him something to eat when nobody was watching. After being warned repeatedly to leave the alligator alone, Mom walked out one afternoon and emptied the cylinder of a .22 caliber revolver on that little gator. I don't know if she hit him. It could be she just wanted to scare him away. Either way, we never saw him again. That day, my brother and I learned that we had best not press our luck with Dolores Pappy Rentz.

Another vivid memory from my childhood was going to the Jacksonville Zoo and to the alligator farm in St. Augustine. I understand it is now called the St. Augustine Alligator Farm Zoological Park on Anastasia Island. It is one of the oldest attractions around St. Augustine, tracing its roots back to the early 1890's. Pappy was very adept at yelping up wild turkeys and even better at grunting up alligators (mama calling babies, babies calling mama, and a bull gator bellowing to attract a female). Once Pappy started grunting up alligators at the Jacksonville Zoo or at the St. Augustine Alligator Farm, it woke them up and disturbed them. It didn't take long for a zookeeper or an alligator wrestler to politely ask that the visitors not disturb the wildlife. I remember Pappy flashing a big smile as we would beg him to continue to call the gators.

Alligator hunting for sport became illegal in Florida in 1962. Alligators were put on the Endangered Species List in 1967. Pappy had been on hundreds of hunts with his father, Robert, as a child and as a young man. Pappy was thirty-five years old when Robert died in 1945. He had Alzheimer's disease, which Pappy called the hardening of the arteries of the brain.

Pappy was a picky eater and didn't care for alligator meat, perhaps because he had eaten so much of it growing up. Gatorin' was done out of necessity and not just for the meat or hides. In the culture I grew up in, wayward alligators and varmints would usually die of "lead poisoning" (getting shot by the landowner). Sometimes people would call Pappy to remove or relocate a confused gator who had wandered into the yard and had gotten too close to the house or the livestock.

Pappy continued gatorin' throughout most of his life. I am fairly sure that Pappy was never officially licensed, but I know that he taught game wardens how to catch and handle alligators. It was the game wardens who would call on Pappy when a gator showed up in the wrong place. Although they were considered endangered from 1967 until

1987, there were always plenty of alligators around where we lived.

When I was between eight and twelve years old, I would accompany Pappy on alligator calls. I was only allowed to watch him as he gave instruction throughout the capture. He did the catching, noosing, and taping of the alligator. Once secured, I helped him drag the gator and put it in the truck or trailer. By the time I was old enough to actually assist in the capture or catch of a larger alligator, Pappy had all but given up his job as the one people could call with an alligator problem. One of my regrets in life was that, as an older teenager, I was only able to accompany Pappy fewer than ten times to watch him and actually assist him in doing what he did so well. I probably learned as much from the "Pappyisms" he passed down to me as from observing the master at work. I do remember watching him grunt up a big bull gator that was getting into people's livestock, then quietly and gently placing a cattle lasso around his neck. The gator never flinched until he realized he was caught. Once the noose tightened, the alligator went into the "death roll." They always go into the death roll, no matter how big or small, once they realize they are caught. Looking back, I consider Pappy to have been a true alligator whisperer.

As I got older and began playing high school sports and dating, I made fewer trips to the farm. One of the saddest days of my life was when I had to sell my horse, which I kept at the farm, because Pappy was selling and downsizing. He and Nanny moved to a smaller house which he built across the road. At the new house, he had his garden and continued to keep bees, but his horse Nellie and the rest of the livestock were gone. Nanny told us that he wept when he had to sell Nellie. I cannot remember ever seeing Pappy cry. Before I graduated from high school, Pappy had totally retired from hunting, trapping critters, and catching snakes and alligators. I suppose that he knew when it was time to walk away from the things he loved and had done most of his life. It must be incredibly difficult to realize you are not as strong or as quick or as focused as you once were, especially when it is a high risk activity. It is even worse to not recognize and acknowledge it.

Nanny died in 1984, two days after Christmas. After Nanny's death, Pappy began to have issues with dementia and eventually Alzheimer's disease like his father, Robert. Tragically, Pappy spent the last five years of his life in a nursing home not knowing or recognizing anyone. My mother, Dolores, died of Alzheimer's disease in 2015. Alzheimer's disease is the one "family tradition" that I hope and pray to avoid.

CHAPTER THREE
Run and Gun

I went to college after graduating from high school. After a couple of half-hearted years, I dropped out, vowing I would never go to college again. I then chased some dreams, including trying to make it as a professional golfer. That didn't go so well. I once played in a three-day tournament where I shot rounds of 69, 72, and 94. I was clearly a schizophrenic golfer who could shoot in the 60's one day, the 70's the next, and the 90's the next. I worked several different jobs including bartending and working at a nuclear power plant while trying to play golf. In 1984 at age twenty-eight, after failing to qualify for the U.S. Open, which had been my goal, I put everything behind me and went in a different direction. I answered what I felt was a call to ministry, something I had been fighting for 10 years. I got married and went back to college. This time I was focused, committed, and driven.

I began serving my first congregation as an assistant

pastor in 1985. I went on to earn my Bachelor's and Master's degrees. I was ordained as a Deacon in 1989 and later as an Elder in Full Connection in 1992 in the Florida Conference of the United Methodist Church. I had clearly been the victim of a praying grandmother. I blame Nanny Pappy, while at the same time giving her the credit for praying me into the ministry where I served as a pastor for thirty-nine years.

I was blessed with three sons: Caleb (1988), Cody (1990), and Keyton (1997). I was blessed with a great wife, but our marriage ended after seventeen years. Ministry is tough on any marriage. A couple of years later, in August of 2003, God brought Marcia into my life. When she agreed to go gatorin' with me on the third date, I knew she was my soul mate (more on that story later!). I married her in September 2004. I became a stepfather to Josh and Alaina. Marcia continues to put up with me after twenty-two years!

I had a wonderful career, and evidently it was successful because every church I served grew under my leadership. When I retired in June of 2024, the congregation I had been serving for ten years had grown to the second largest United Methodist Church in the Florida Conference.

I studied at Emory University under Dr. Fred Craddock and adopted his style of inductive, narrative, "storytelling" preaching. This style is not "preachy" or the old "3 points and a prayer" style, but rather encourages and allows the listener to discover and arrive at the message of the sermon. Ten different people may reach ten different conclusions, which could all be correct. My hope was always that they would remember the message and still be discussing it over lunch after church. Storytelling comes naturally to me—an inherited gift.

Throughout my younger adult life to this point, the memories of Pappy and my early life as a wannabe alligator hunting cracker never truly faded away. However, I never could have imagined that I would be able to legally hunt alligators. In 1987, Florida alligators were removed from the Endangered Species List. Much to my surprise and joy, alligator tag lottery hunts began through Florida's Statewide Alligator Harvest Program in 1988. You could apply for hunts in different harvest areas (or zones) and dates. I applied, of course, and was often chosen. According to the latest information online, more than 15,000 applicants will apply for 7,000 permits. The season runs from August 15 to November 1 each year. It is strictly regulated, and firearms are not allowed to be carried.

It was through these lottery hunts that I was able to legally hunt alligators in the exact area where my parents' lake house was located on Lake George. They sold the house and property many years before, but I was still familiar with the lake. I had grown up fishing in my harvest area, and it was the exact place where Pappy had taken me for my first night of gatorin'. It was where I caught and released small gators as a child.

During the years I was assigned as the Senior Pastor of Cape Coral First United Methodist Church, I got to know a man in the church by the name of Olin. To this very day, Olin is one of my true heroes. I would go so far as to place him among the top five men I have ever known. Through conversations, Olin learned of my love for alligator hunting, and I told him about my family's history with alligators. Olin and his wife, Florence, had a lake house near Lake Istokpoga. Olin not only loved to hunt alligators, but he loved to hunt alligators by airboat. I was invited to join him, his son-in-law Scott (who also owned an airboat), and a group of incredible alligator hunters. Olin and Florence literally made me feel like family. For the next several years, I applied for tags for Lake Istokpoga and truly had some of the best times of my entire life. Lake Istokpoga is a very large, shallow, muddy lake, and some huge alligators have been taken from the lake over the years.

One year, Scott had T-shirts made up for this gang of alligator hunters. I still have mine, and it reads, "Gator Squad 2003 - Saving the World, One Gator at a Time." Scott also put together a video of the gang. Everyone was given a nickname. The "Gator Squad" consisted of Action Jackson, E.T., The Lawyer, Big Olin, Ice Man, Pops, Lucky, Bird Dog, Bang Stick, Fat Truck Driver… and me, The Preacher. The hunts were not allowed to start until sunset. We would hunt all through the night until daylight. After a few days into the season, however, the gators become very wary and didn't even show themselves.

The airboat captain drives the boat and wears a headlamp. The person hunting is seated behind the captain, holding a long aluminum pole equipped with a breakaway dart and a rope with a float. When the captain spots the eyes of the alligator, he makes a run toward the gator, reaching speeds up to 30-40 mph. That is where the term "Run and Gun" (gunning the throttle when an alligator is spotted) is from. The captain tries to keep the light off the gator until the last possible second so that the gator will not go under the water. When the gator is boatside, it is the job of the hunter to "stick" the alligator with the dart at a high rate of speed. You never throw the pole but rather let the power and force of the airboat embed the breakaway dart into the alligator. It definitely takes some practice, along with a little bit of luck. I actually stuck a six-foot, eight-inch gator on the first night I ever tried it, but there are always a ton of misses.

There is nothing quite as exhilarating, after you've stuck one, as when the captain turns the airboat around and you see the float making a wake through the water, with a stuck alligator on the line. To be successful, the captain and hunter must be in sync. I found that I did very well with Scott and Fat Truck Driver, but with some captains, I couldn't stick an elephant. It wasn't the captain's fault. Some captain-hunter teams mesh, and some just don't. It can be very frustrating at times.

I have never experienced being around such amazing people; the times of chasing, sticking, and catching alligators were out of this world. The experience of flying through the swamps, marshes, and open water on an airboat, all while swallowing bugs and being blinded by mosquitoes pelting you in the face, is truly unforgettable. I probably have a hundred stories from those amazing, fun nights, but I will only share a few here.

Airboats typically hold the captain, who sits in the front seat and two people behind. Occasionally you see an airboat where the captain is in the back seat and passengers are in the front. Every airboat I hunted in had the captain in the front, which I think is better for alligator hunting. One night we were hunting with Fat Truck Driver as captain, Olin sitting next to me, and I was the hunter. It was fairly early in the hunt, around 10-11 p.m., when Fat Truck Driver spotted a gator and gunned the throttle. I got in position, leaned over and got ready to stick the gator. It was a swampy area with a lot of cover. At the very moment I tried to stick the gator, Fat Truck Driver hit a floating tussock (a natural island of vegetation). The airboat went airborne, and I flew out, getting a glimpse of the bottom of the airboat as I flipped head over heels. Being an excellent and experienced driver, Fat Truck Driver accelerated to keep the airboat flying. Had he let off the gas with the airboat airborne, it could have easily flipped.

    By the time I got my bearings, I was able to stand up, but only to see the airboat lights continuing straight into the distance. Fat Truck Driver didn't realize that I was no longer in the airboat, and Olin didn't realize that Fat Truck Driver was unaware. I suddenly came to the realization that I had tried to stick an alligator, had no idea where he was or if he was stuck, and I was now in the place where he was just seconds before! It seemed like forever (which was in reality only a couple of minutes) that I stood there in chest deep water, in the pure darkness, waiting for Fat Truck Driver and Olin to find me.

    Even though I was soaked, we never went back so I could change clothes, because all I wanted to do was get back to hunting. From that night on, when I hunted with Olin next to me, he held on to the back of my belt so that I would not get thrown out again! Olin once played football for the Green Bay Packers and was strong. He made sure I stayed safe. My flipping out of a flying airboat into the water with an alligator became an inside joke about Velcro among the Gator Squad.

Olin was always so gracious in allowing me to bring friends and occasionally one of my children to have an airboat hunting experience. When I met and started dating Marcia, she couldn't wrap her head around this gator hunting thing. I figured I would break her in early or lose her altogether when I invited her to go "Run and Gun" alligators. It literally was our third official date. Marcia has a real sense of adventure and didn't complain about the bugs. She immediately loved Fat Truck Driver. She loaded up on coffee, knowing that we would probably be out all night. A couple hours into the hunt, she tapped Fat Truck Driver on the back and said we needed to take her back because she had to use the bathroom. We were near one of the islands in Lake Istokpoga, so Fat Truck Driver pulled the airboat up on the island and spun it around.

"Here?" Marcia asked as she climbed out of the airboat onto the overgrown island, and then asked if there were any snakes on the island.

"Snakes, huge spiders, alligators, wild hogs," was Fat Truck Driver's reply.

"Well, I have to pee," she said.

"Then go ahead and pee," he replied.

"Are you going to look?" she asked.

"Probably," he replied. "And if you don't hurry up, I will put the spotlight on you."

That was the last time we stopped on the island. For

the rest of the night, Marcia just became one of the guys and positioned her bottom over the side of the airboat whenever we stopped for a pee break. She never complained and had the time of her life. I realized that I had found a keeper.

Ten years after that, we were "Run and Gun" hunting on Lake Kissimmee with another friend of mine who had an airboat. Marcia stuck an eleven-foot-two-inch trophy gator. Not only did she stick it, but she also dispensed it with a knife because the bang stick didn't work.

You're not allowed to have a firearm, like a pistol or a rifle on a quota hunt even if you are a licensed trapper. The captured alligator must be dispatched as quickly as possible. A bang stick is the preferred method. Bang sticks are also called powerheads. They are basically a pole with a chamber at the end that holds a live ammunition cartridge against a firing pin. It is detonated when pushed hard against your target. They are mainly used for alligators or sharks. Technically, they are still a firearm. Nuisance trappers are allowed to have a pistol and rifle and use them from time to time while carrying out their duties, however, you must first obtain permission from SNAP and notify local law enforcement if you are in a populated area.

After Marcia caught her first alligator, I asked her if she was happy. Her comment was that she would never be happy until she got a bigger one than me. Did I happen to mention how competitive she is?

Throughout the night of a hunt, airboats stayed in communication with each other by cell phone. There are usually at least three boats on the water at any given time. Sometimes they might need help or sometimes we just took breaks together. I will never forget the night that someone had stuck an alligator on another airboat. We pulled up fairly close to them as they followed the float and eventually brought the alligator alongside their airboat. I don't remember exactly who dispatched the alligator with the bang stick. What I vividly remember is that blood began to gush from Lucky's head. Instead of hitting the kill zone with the bang stick, the bullet hit the bone that is just in front of the kill zone, which caused pieces of bone to fly through the air. A sharp piece of bone hit Lucky in the head. He wasn't hurt, but he was bleeding profusely from the head wound. That is one reason we always wear safety goggles; they are not just for keeping the bugs out of your eyes. After everyone realized Lucky would be OK and the bleeding stopped, the catch line of that evening was, "Lucky got lucky."

I have gotten several twelve-foot-plus alligators as a nuisance trapper, but one of my biggest alligators (overall length, not weight) came while "Run and Gun" hunting with Scott and Fat Truck Driver. Ironically, we were not up and running fast, but going rather slowly, gently gliding through some very shallow water. Fat Truck Driver was shining his headlight straight down into the black, murky water, when just a couple of feet under the water, the back of a very large alligator appeared. I reacted instinctively and slammed the dart into his back as hard as I could. The alligator created a wake when he took off, and the chase was on! Within thirty minutes we hit him with the bang stick and had to drag him to a shallow area to load him into the airboat. Of course, we always tape the mouth closed just in case. Scott videotaped the experience. It took some maneuvering and help from another boat to load a twelve-foot-three-inch, 500-pound dead alligator into an airboat. The airboat's gunwale was barely inches above the water without any extra weight. It was a slow, easy ride to the marina where a crane was used to unload the behemoth. It was truly the gator of a lifetime. I have a mount of his head on my wall. I named him Henry. One of the guys we hunted with named Elmer, or E.T. as we called him, had stuck a very large alligator the week before. Something happened where the line holding the breakaway dart came loose. After careful examination that night, we found Elmer's dart with that broken line in the twelve-foot-three-inch, 500-pound gator I brought in.

    I suppose my favorite story from the "Run and Gun" days involved Scott taking me out on the very last night of the season. I still had a tag to burn and had not been able to get away to hunt very much like in years past. Scott is a great driver, and he and I work well together. We began hunting at sunset, and I told him I needed to be back at my truck by 4:30 a.m. I needed to have time to make the two-hour drive back to Bradenton so I could get home to shower, change clothes, and be at church ready to preach for the 8:30 a.m. and 11:00 a.m. services.

    It was one of those nights when the gators were not showing. I literally didn't have anything to attempt a stick the entire night. It was 4 a.m., and we were down to our last thirty minutes of hunting. My truck was parked in Olin's yard, thirty minutes away by boat. As Scott turned the airboat to head towards the truck, he saw an alligator eye breaking the surface about sixty yards away over his right shoulder. As he made a hard right turn and gunned the airboat accelerator, I got ready to make the stick. The gator boiled the surface and went under about ten to fifteen yards before we got to him. I pointed and released the stick pole into the swirling water. Both Scott and I knew by the sound that I had hit something. The rope and float flew out of the boat, and the chase was on!

The gator was going at such a speed that it was obviously a large one. Eventually, we got him up to the boat and hit him with the bang stick. He was a lot larger than we expected.

Scott and I had no one to help us get him into the boat. We ended up dragging him to a shallow place where we were able to get out and roll him into the airboat for a slow ride to my truck. I glanced at the time. It was 4:45 a.m., and I should have been on the road fifteen minutes earlier. Now we had to get back and somehow get the alligator from the airboat and load him into my truck to drop him off at Parker Brothers Cooler and Alligator Processors. Best case scenario, if everything went perfectly, I would be an hour and a half behind schedule. I would have to skip the shower and just have Marcia meet me at church with a change of clothes and try to clean up with a washcloth and a towel in my office bathroom.

Once we got back to my truck, Scott and I were able to get the airboat on his trailer and then pull it with his truck up beside mine. We rolled the alligator out of the airboat and into the bed of my truck. That old bull alligator measured eleven feet, four inches.

Thankfully, there was someone at Parker Brothers

to help me drag the gator into the cooler. It was now after 6:30 a.m., and I had a two-hour drive to make it to the first worship service that began at 8:30 a.m.

I looked down at myself. My clothes were very bloody from having to bear-hug the gator while loading and unloading him. An old bull gator has an unmistakable stench that takes a lot of soap and water to scrub off. I smelled terrible!

Nevertheless, I jumped in my truck and picked up State Road 70 between Okeechobee and US Highway 27, headed west towards Arcadia and then on to Bradenton. I am not, and never have been, a habitual speeder. If anything, Marcia and the kids always accuse me of driving too slow. On this early morning, though, I was pushing the limit, driving 80-85 mph in a 60 mph zone. Around ten miles east of Arcadia, there is a prison and a state trooper substation. I figured I would slow down when I went through that area. However, before I realized it, I was suddenly face to face with a state trooper heading eastbound before I could think about slowing down. My speed was 85 mph. I saw him spin around and hit his blue lights.

I pulled over and had the window rolled down when he walked up and put the flashlight in my face. There I sat with smelly, blood-covered clothes. He shined the light in the bed of my truck, and there was obvious blood from the alligator.

"License and registration," he said, along with, "What in the hell have you been up to, and why are you in such a hurry?"

"Sir," I replied, "I have been alligator hunting on

Lake Istokpoga. It was the last night of the season, and I stuck a big gator late. I have to get to Bradenton by 8:30 a.m. because I am a pastor and gotta preach this morning."

He stood there looking at me with his flashlight in my face and started laughing out loud. "I'll tell you, that has to be the best one I have ever heard... you are a preacher... yep, that is truly the very best speeding excuse that I have ever heard, and I don't believe you," he said.

"I am not lying, sir," I pleaded.

"What proof do you have that you are a preacher? With all that blood all over you I should probably just take you straight to jail. Hell, you could have just killed somebody," he said.

"Sir, on my passenger seat I have a bulletin from my church. Here is my name, same as on my license, and I also have my sermon right here," I said as I handed it to him.

He looked it over and handed it back to me. "I am not going to give you a ticket since you are a preacher running late to church, but you drive the speed limit the rest of the way. If you are late, they can sing until you get there. You just need to get there safely. And if I ever catch you speeding again on my road here, I will throw the book at you. And... by the way, you smell terrible, son. You best get a bath before you get to church. Now get the hell out of here and be careful," he said.

I thanked him and headed towards Bradenton. I made it to the church about fifteen minutes late. Despite my best efforts with soap and a washcloth in my office bathroom, I could not rid myself of the smell. For some strange reason, no one stood in line to shake my hand after church that morning after I shared my reason for being late and for smelling the way I did.

By the way, I also have the mount of this bull alligator's head, and I still have his beautiful, tanned hide. I will never part with the memories of that night, the hunt, Scott maneuvering the airboat and putting me in position to stick the swirling alligator, the state trooper, and arriving late for church on a Sunday morning covered with alligator blood and stench. There's nothing like running and gunning! It's truly exhilarating.

CHAPTER FOUR
Friends

I always looked forward to Florida's Statewide Alligator Harvest Program each year, which gave me the opportunity to hunt. I also knew about a program called SNAP (Statewide Nuisance Alligator Program) where licensed nuisance alligator trappers in the county were often called on to remove alligators. We were members at River Strand Golf and Country Club in Bradenton, and their driving range was unique in that you hit off the tee and into a lake. On a number of occasions, I would stand on the driving range and watch the nuisance trappers at work. They would remove an alligator by snagging it with a treble hook on a rod and reel, wear it out, and then slip a noose around its neck. Once the alligator was secured on shore, its mouth was taped shut. It was put into a truck or trailer and taken away. I often thought what a great job that must be, but it never entered my mind to apply to be a part of the program.

I can't begin to tell you how surprised I was when I

received information in the mail inviting me to apply to be an FWC (Florida Wildlife Commission) Licensed Nuisance Alligator Trapper for Manatee County. I am not sure how they got my name, but I was told they contacted me because I had been active in the harvest program hunts. It almost seemed too good to be true. Would I be qualified? Would I have enough time to do the job? I was already working forty-plus hours a week pastoring a congregation in Bradenton.

I looked up the qualifications online: you must reside near your assigned trapping area, possess email capability, demonstrate a commitment to customer service, adhere to fish and wildlife regulations, have no wildlife violations on your record, have a clean criminal history, project a positive image to the public and the media, and have your own equipment (such as a truck, trailer, snares, hooks, rods, and whatever else you need for capturing an alligator). I had everything so far. The big question for me was the qualification that said that you must have availability and flexibility to respond to your duties. The priorities I always try to live by are God first, family second, and church third. As a full-time pastor, I really wasn't allowed to have another job. However, what if I were to call this opportunity "community service," instead of looking at it as another job? I reconciled this question thinking that I could do it as long as I kept my priorities in order. I could always find a free hour here or there. The leadership of the church I was serving gave their permission for me to pursue this "community service."

I applied and was invited to an interview in Manatee County with people from Tallahassee as well as the SNAP director in Okeechobee. I was offered the position pending background checks, training, orientation, and the successful completion of a written exam. There were four of us who were hired together. We would not only be rookies together, but we would also be the only licensed trappers in Manatee County. As of 2025, an estimated 464,000 people call Manatee County home. This marks a 44% increase since 2010 and has had a direct impact on pushing alligators out of their natural habitats. Covering more than 890 square miles, the county sits on Florida's west coast—about an hour south of Tampa and just north of Sarasota. It's a place where there are beautiful beaches along the coast, and working cattle ranches in the eastern part of the county. There are numerous subdivisions throughout the county, with 30 named lakes and countless stormwater and residential ponds scattered throughout the landscape. One of the new trapper hires didn't last a month, so essentially there were three of us rookie trappers covering the entire county.

It was at the orientation and training session that I met Kevin. There are some people that you meet and immediately do not like. You are not sure why you don't like them, but you just don't. On the other hand, sometimes you meet a person and you immediately like them. Kevin was one of those people. He was from Braidwood, a small town in Illinois. He owned a sporting goods store and was Deputy Fire Chief before moving to Florida. Like me, Kevin loved to hunt and fish. I found out that he also participated in the alligator harvest hunts. Kevin and I hit it off immediately. We also got along with Mike F., the third trapper who was hired. We all liked the fourth guy, although no one was surprised when he resigned after the first month.

Mike acquired a designated agent whose name was Brandon. Designated agents assist the alligator trapper with the duties and responsibilities of the position. Brandon was great, and the four of us got along well. Mike and Brandon were a natural team. Kevin and I likewise made a great team. We all helped and covered for each other. A couple of years after we started, another trapper by the name of Robert was hired. I also think the world of Robert. He is another guy, like Kevin, who is honest, trustworthy, and always there to help you. Robert is big and strong, literally one of the toughest people I have ever met. He is a tenacious trapper, and I don't think the guy is afraid of anything. He whupped cancer, and there isn't an alligator that exists that Robert can't bring down. Robert is another guy who has stepped up and helped me on so many occasions. I truly enjoyed the alligator permits we have worked together and the gators we have caught. I thank God for Robert and his friendship.

I have always covered my smaller alligator permits individually, and Kevin has always done the same. However, it didn't take us long to figure out that we were much more successful working as a team on the alligators that were eight feet and longer.

Kevin is a very likeable guy, and he is easy to be around. You hardly ever see the guy without a big smile on his face. He takes gatorin' very seriously and is an excellent trapper. He goes strictly by the rules and is safety minded. He is someone you can always count on to be there for you. A couple of months after we were hired and had begun to work some permits together, my oldest son, Caleb, blew the transmission in his car in Naples while towing his boat to the Keys. He had just gotten out of the Army. I called Kevin and asked if I could borrow his flatbed trailer to tow my son's car back home. Kevin immediately took his truck and trailer, driving to Naples to pick up Caleb and his car. I followed, towing his boat back with my truck. Kevin refused to take a dime, not even money to cover fuel. That shows what kind of friend he is. I can't count the number of times he has helped me out over the years.

One summer in the Florida Keys, he put his dinner on hold to help me change a flat inside dually tire on my truck with the boat already in tow. He helped to get us on the road with a horrible thunderstorm bearing down. There have been a couple of times that I observed people taking advantage of Kevin's good nature. I discovered that if you ever screw him over, he is done with you.

Early on, Marcia and I met Kevin's beautiful wife, Julie. What a perfect couple! Over the years, we have enjoyed spending summer vacations with them in the Keys, including fishing and diving with them. We have shared meals in each other's homes and count them among the closest and best friends we have. They adopted one of our Labrador puppies from a litter we bred and named him Bentley. Marcia and I have two of Bentley's sisters, Sansa and Khali.

I take the time to write and share this chapter detailing my friendship with Kevin because it would be impossible for me to write a book about gatorin' without including Kevin. He and I have literally caught hundreds of alligators together and have had so many unforgettable calls, experiences, and permits. Now that we are both retired from our regular jobs, we spend even more time together, often just riding along with each other whether we need help or not. In the next chapter of this book, I will share several detailed gatorin' stories about some of the permits we worked together. I often think back to the day I met Kevin. I am so thankful that God allowed our lives and paths to cross. It is rare in today's world to have friends like Kevin and Robert. They are like brothers to me, and I know we will be friends for the rest of our lives. Kevin and Robert are not just good people, they are the best trappers I know!

CHAPTER FIVE
Gatorin' as a Nuisance Alligator Trapper

I am one of 103 contracted Nuisance Alligator Trappers (NAT) in Florida. Many of us have Licensed Trapping Agents working with us and under our direct supervision. If someone believes that an alligator poses a threat to people, pets, or property, they are encouraged to call the SNAP (State Nuisance Alligator Program) hotline. The Florida Fish and Wildlife Conservation Commission (FWC) provides a toll-free number, 866-FWC-GATOR (866-392-4286). The SNAP office is located in Okeechobee, Florida. If the complaint meets qualifying criteria, SNAP will issue a permit to a NAT.

Generally, an alligator may be considered a nuisance if it is at least four feet in length. Alligators less than four feet are not considered to be large enough to be dangerous to people or pets unless handled. Complainants must be able to grant legal access to the property on which the alligator is located. SNAP does not issue a permit for the removal of alligators from private or publicly managed property without first obtaining permission from the property owner or management authority. Occasionally, local law enforcement will contact a NAT after working hours to respond to an eCall (emergency call). These calls are especially common during the months of April through June, which is mating season, when alligators are the most active. If an alligator is captured after hours as a result of an LE (law enforcement) call, it is documented, and a permit is issued when the SNAP office opens. The many deputies that I have worked with over the years have all been very helpful and supportive.

I would like to say how appreciative I am for the staff and leadership at SNAP. I have always found them to be extremely helpful. They truly go out of their way when working with the nuisance alligator trappers. Dealing with people regarding the presence of an alligator cannot be an easy job, and the SNAP personnel do it with dignity and grace.

Once an alligator is captured, there is a significant amount of paperwork to be done by the trapper. Alligator Harvest Report Forms (AHRF) record the size and sex of the alligator, exactly when and where it was captured, exactly what was done with the alligator after capture, and its CITES (Convention on International Trade in Endangered Species) tag. All alligators are given a CITES tag except for captured gators which are under four feet. These small alligators are relocated. A Live Transfer Form is required if the captured alligator is sold alive to a licensed alligator farm. This paperwork is sent to the SNAP office each month by every NAT. Every captured alligator must be accounted for and there is a paper trail which follows it. Often, the paperwork takes more time than the capture itself.

Once someone feeds a wild alligator, they begin to associate people with food. I recently responded to a complaint that an alligator was approaching people. I arrived at the site and walked down to the water to get an idea of the actual size of the alligator. A five-foot alligator, who was across the pond from where I was standing, spotted me and made a beeline, swimming right toward me. I walked back to my truck to grab a rod and reel with a treble hook and a noose. I quickly headed back to the pond to discover that the alligator had, in fact, climbed out of the pond and was following me to my truck. By the time I got to him, he was halfway between the pond and my truck. Obviously, this alligator had been fed, and his behavior was unusually aggressive even for a fed alligator. I walked up to him, and he stood his ground. I actually said to him in jest, "Okay, buddy. I will go open the door of my truck and you can just climb in." I slipped the noose around his neck, caught him, taped his mouth shut, and put him in my trailer.

There is an old saying, "There are no nuisance alligators, just nuisance people." There is some truth to that, but not entirely. I say to people every day, "Never, ever feed an alligator!" There are also many cases where an alligator that has never been fed shows up at the front door, in a swimming pool, on the highway, or even at a local store. The building of so many new homes and subdivisions has definitely driven alligators from their natural habitat where they have roamed free for generations. But alligators would find and kill livestock and show up in strange places even when Pappy and his father, Robert, were trapping one hundred years ago. I have personally worked permits in the northeastern part of Manatee County, a rural area where alligators were eating calves.

This chapter is a compilation of a number of gatorin' experiences I have had while working permits as a Nuisance Alligator Trapper. Every capture has its own story. The following stories are some of my favorites and are factual events that have not been embellished.

Back in the spring of 2012, I responded to a permit to remove a very large alligator that was showing aggressive behavior towards golfers on a golf course. The alligator was in a pond next to the green on hole 14.

I had to park my truck a good distance from the pond and walk to where the alligator was located. As I walked up, I saw a golfer bent over with his club in the water, trying to retrieve a golf ball. He didn't notice the very large alligator swimming towards him. I hollered and pointed, and the golfer scrambled up the bank. He thanked me and moved on to the next hole. This alligator was one of the largest ones I had ever encountered. It was late in the afternoon, but one lesson I had learned early on: get the alligator while he is there and you are there; otherwise, there is a good chance that he will move on and become someone else's nuisance.

I was aware that it would be dark in an hour, and I definitely needed help with this one. Kevin had been out of town hunting and was on his way back. I gave him a call, but he said he was still an hour away. He suggested that I go ahead and get a hook in the alligator, and he would be there as soon as he could. He said he would bring Rooster, one of his trapping agents who was with him (it was years later that I found out Rooster's real name was Ryan). I told Kevin to also bring his trailer to put the alligator in once we caught him. I went to my truck and grabbed a couple of rods and reels with treble hooks, covered myself with bug spray, and grabbed my headlamp.

It was an easy cast into the pond and hook-up because there was a lot of alligator to work with. He made a couple of runs and then settled down into the mud in the middle of the pond. I sat on the bank with a tight line waiting on Kevin and Rooster. A few of the golf course staff came out to check on me and volunteered the use of a golf cart to pull the gator out when we got him close to shore. Kevin and Rooster eventually arrived, and before either one of them could get a second hook in him, somehow my hook came out. It was a sick feeling, thinking I had just lost this massive, aggressive alligator after holding him for so long. A few minutes later, Rooster made a blind cast to the middle of the pond and hooked him. Kevin and I made subsequent casts and also hooked him. With three hooks now in him, we were able to pull him close enough to get a noose around him.

Once noosed, he put up a fight. It wasn't for long, though, because bigger gators tend to tire out more quickly. As we pulled him to shore, Rooster was insistent on being the one to tape his mouth shut. We always use electrical tape for the job and never duct tape because it comes off too easily. Rooster went crazy with the tape, using twice as much as was needed. That night, the phrase "go Rooster on him" was born, and it means using more tape than what is necessary to secure the gator's mouth. To this day, when we catch a big alligator, Kevin or I will say, "Be sure and go Rooster on him!"

Mind you, it was already dark when Kevin and Rooster arrived, so we had been working in total darkness using just our headlamps. After Rooster taped the gator's mouth, I called the staff member who volunteered a golf cart. One thing I learned that night was that a golf cart does not have enough power to pull a twelve-foot-plus alligator up a bank and out of the water. Even with all of us pushing the golf cart and pulling on the 500-pound alligator, it was futile. Kevin had to unhook his trailer, make the twenty-minute drive to his house to get his 4-wheeler, and come back. Thankfully, his 4-wheeler easily pulled the alligator out of the pond and to where the trailer was parked. It took Kevin, Rooster, and me, plus a few golf course staff members to get the alligator loaded. He was huge!

I realized that almost six hours had passed since I had arrived at the pond. I remember being totally exhausted and very hungry. The alligator measured twelve feet, six inches. I have his head mounted on the wall in our guest house, next to the twelve-foot-three inch alligator I got at Lake Istokpoga.

Whenever the story of this alligator comes up and Rooster is anywhere around, he makes the claim that this was his alligator. He says he was the one who hooked it after my hook came out, and he was the one to tape the alligator's mouth shut. According to Rooster, it was clearly his alligator. I have had to remind Rooster it was my permit, my initial hookup, my name was on the Alligator Harvest Report Form (AHRF), and the alligator's head is on my wall. I would never have been able to get this alligator without Kevin and Rooster. Seriously, it took all of us to catch this beast. I came back to the golf course the next day and removed an almost eight-foot-long female gator by myself from the same pond.

I once responded to a call by a man who had recently moved to Manatee County from New York. The permit issued by the SNAP office listed the alligator as ten feet in length. When I walked around the complainant's house to his back yard, I commented that he had a very small pond to hold a ten-foot alligator. He readily admitted that he had not yet seen the alligator and had just estimated the size.

"How did you come up with ten feet?" I asked.

"Well, he sounds like he is at least ten feet," he replied.

He explained that he had only heard the gator. About that time a bullfrog began to croak.

"There he is! There he is! Do you hear him?" he joyfully asked me.

"Sir, that is not an alligator, that is a bullfrog," I told him.

He suddenly became enraged. How dare I suggest that the noise was not a ten-foot alligator?!

"You have no idea what you are talking about, and you call yourself an alligator trapper?" he shouted at me. "Listen buddy, I have watched a lot of nature shows on TV and I know what an alligator sounds like," he shouted, as his face became red with anger.

"Sir," I responded, "I am a native Floridian, and I can assure you that the sound you are hearing is a bullfrog and not an alligator," trying to reason with him.

He then invited me, using a tirade of four-letter words, to leave his property and not return until I could learn the difference between the sound of a bullfrog and the sound of a ten-foot alligator. I think it is safe to say that he never actually saw that ten-foot alligator that sounded exactly like a bullfrog.

On a lighter note, I once had a permit near the community of Parrish. The complainant was an older lady who lived with her husband on ten acres with a beautiful, well-maintained pond. She explained that there was an alligator in the pond which was about five feet long and showed no fear of humans. I retreated to my truck to get a rod and a noose. I also brought my boom box that has recordings of a mama gator calling babies and babies calling back. These recordings will sometimes draw an alligator toward the sound. I played the recording, expecting to see the alligator swimming toward me any second. The lady stood there looking at me inquisitively.

Finally, she asked, "What are you doing?"

I explained that I was trying to call the alligator so I could catch it. "Do you want me to call the alligator?" she asked.

"Do you know how to call an alligator?" I replied.

"Sure do. I call him over here all the time," and she began, "Here little gator, here, here, here, here little gator, gator, gator."

I seriously thought she was making a joke until the

alligator came out from where he was hiding and swam toward us. I had never seen anything like it! After the gator was caught and put in the trailer, her husband let me in on the secret. She had been feeding the koi and bream every evening for years, calling them up with, "Here fishy, fishy, fishy." About two years earlier this alligator showed up when he was very small. She had been calling and feeding him ever since. Unfortunately, the alligator had begun to eat her beautiful, expensive koi. He was getting too big and aggressive, so she knew he had to go.

I am a dog lover. Dogs have always been a big part of my life. I have told close friends that I like dogs more than I like most people. Unfortunately, alligators also love dogs. I can't begin to tell you how many permits I have responded to that were dog-related. In most cases, the dog got too close to the water and was grabbed by the alligator. Kevin and I used to see a couple who lived near him walk their two Boston Terriers every day. One evening around sunset, a very large alligator came out of the water and nabbed one of the dogs. Kevin and I worked the permit to catch the gator. We caught a ten-foot gator and took it to a processor in Plant City who, upon opening the alligator, found the remains of the Boston Terrier. I can't think of too many things more devastating than watching your dog get snatched and killed by an alligator.

I was working a permit one night with my oldest son, Caleb, and one of his lifelong friends, Matt. Caleb is also a big dog lover. The pond we were working was long and narrow and in a relatively new subdivision where there were only a few houses. We stood at one end of the pond and played the alligator calls on my boom box. From the other end of the pond, we heard a big splash from something entering the water. I walked toward the splash and saw a dog swimming toward us, right down the middle of the pond. About ten yards behind the dog, I saw the red eyes of an alligator that was bearing down on the dog. We ran as fast as we could toward the dog, with Caleb getting there first. He didn't hesitate to wade out into the water, calling and coaxing the dog to swim toward him. The alligator went under at about the same time that Caleb got to the dog. He was standing in chest deep water holding the dog. The alligator was somewhere nearby.

Matt and I got into the water and helped Caleb pull the dog up the bank to safety. As I watched things unfold, I was first in fear for the dog, but then I was in fear for my son. But I know I would have done the same thing to save the dog. The dog was a big, beautiful, male golden retriever. We went back to where the truck was parked, knowing we now had to find the golden retriever's home. As we all stood there, wet and assessing everything that just happened, a man walked up to us and said, "Hey, that is my dog," as if we were trying to take it. I recounted to the man what had just happened.

"Well, he gets out and goes swimming all the time," was his only response. There was no "thank you" or show of appreciation for what we had done. I remember saying as he and the dog walked away, "We all risked our lives, especially my son's, to save your dog. That alligator almost had him. You better keep him out of the water, or he might not be so lucky next time."

No response from the man. What did I say about liking dogs more than most people? That guy was one of those "most people." We never saw the gator again that night. On subsequent visits to the pond, we never saw or caught the gator, and we never saw the dog again, either.

I got a law enforcement eCall late one afternoon for an alligator that had pushed through a metal fence, apparently going after a dog. It turns out that a teenage girl was playing with her dog in a fenced backyard and had attracted the alligator's attention. The alligator crawled out of the pond, stuck his nose through the metal fence, and was slowly working on bending it. After more than an hour, the alligator broke through and got into the backyard. The girl, who was home by herself with the dog, had the maturity to call 911 and get inside the house.

Once the alligator got into the backyard, he began to push against the screened-in area off the back of the house called the lanai. He was still pushing on the screen when I arrived. It has always been my experience that a lanai screen is not a challenge for a large gator. Fortunately, I was able to get a noose around him and get his mouth taped shut before he broke through the screen. The alligator measured eight feet, six inches long and was very fat and stocky. I didn't stop to get my trailer on the way to the call, which meant I would have to get him into the bed of my truck to transport him. This was going to be especially difficult because of his size. Unfortunately, on that afternoon I could not reach anyone by phone who could help me. After watching me try to lift and bear-hug this alligator that still wanted to fight, a yard guy, who had arrived to do the lawn, helped me lift him into the bed of my truck. I covered the alligator's eyes and taped all four legs. Using "alligator handcuffs" helps to make the job easier. I secured him down in the bed of my truck for the fifteen-minute ride to my house where I would transfer him to the trailer.

I include this story to show that a fence, whether it be metal, chain link, or privacy, will only slow alligators down, but it will not keep them out. They can go under, climb over, or even go through a fence, especially when dogs and cats are on lanais.

The local news carried the story of a woman in the Tidewater area who was walking her French Bulldog, Frankie, on a leash near the water in her neighborhood around 5:00 a.m. A five-and-a-half-foot alligator came out of the water and grabbed Frankie. The lady yelled, screamed, and tugged on the leash. She was able to wrangle Frankie away from the alligator, but Frankie had numerous wounds. He was taken to the veterinarian, and thankfully he survived. I caught the alligator believed to be the one that grabbed Frankie. This was yet another alligator that showed no fear of people.

Alligators normally feed at night, especially right after dark and right before sunrise. For that reason, it is never smart to walk your pets around a body of water in Florida when it is dark. I ran into Frankie's owner a couple of months after the attack and asked about Frankie. His owner said that he was fine but had so many scars that they had to change his name. He is no longer known as Frankie, they now call him Frankenstein.

One of the questions that I get asked most often

is, "What is the biggest alligator you have ever caught?" I have caught four alligators over twelve feet in length. I have already talked about two of them. The first was in Lake Istokpoga on one of the quota hunts in the airboat. The second was while working as a nuisance trapper in the Rosedale area. The third and fourth were also caught as a trapper working assigned permits.

I was issued a permit to remove a very large alligator that seemed quite interested in the complainant's horse. The complainant lived on Lake Manatee and was quite accustomed to seeing large alligators in her back yard. However, this particular alligator kept inching closer and closer to the barn and the fenced pasture. He seemed to be stalking her horse. He was comfortable moving around the property and didn't appear to be afraid of humans. However, whenever I would show up, he would not be there or he would slip back into the water and disappear. I did not doubt the complainant because she had dozens of pictures to verify that she was telling the truth.

I was still a fairly new trapper, so I did what any new trapper at that time would do: I set a bait. I wanted to catch the alligator before someone or the horse got hurt. The problem with setting a bait in a situation like that is you might not catch the alligator you were targeting. I set the bait late one evening, and the complainant called me at first daylight to let me know the trap had been sprung. She said there seemed to be something on the line. My son, Caleb, accompanied me, and we discovered there was an eight-foot alligator on the line. The line was stretched under the dock and wrapped around a piling.

We discovered that the twelve-foot alligator we were targeting was also under the dock. It had the eight-foot alligator, which was still alive, in his mouth. Even with us walking on the dock just above him, the twelve-foot alligator was not spooked and refused to let go of the eight-foot alligator. I notified the SNAP office, and I was given an "add-on" to my permit. This meant I could now capture both alligators. I also requested a firearm authorization, which I was given. At that time, I carried a Smith .357 revolver and bang stick with .357 and .44 magnum powerheads.

The bang stick would have been perfect except that the twelve-foot alligator had now been able to maneuver the eight-foot alligator several feet away from the dock, stretching the trap line even tighter. I was now unable to reach the twelve-foot alligator with a shot from the bang stick to the "kill zone," the soft part right behind the thick, hard skull bone that encapsulates the brain. We waited a while, but the twelve-foot alligator was not willing to let go of the "smaller" alligator. He was getting increasingly frustrated trying to take his prey with him.

I felt I needed to make a decision to do something one way or the other before the twelve-foot alligator managed to break the trap line. The twelve-foot alligator was now stretched out lengthwise, with his tail still under the dock and his head pointed away. Lying on my stomach with my arms hanging over the edge of the dock, I had a clear, safe shot directly to the kill zone. I took the shot, which appeared to hit the mark. The big alligator quivered, let go of the eight-foot alligator, went under the water for several seconds, and then surfaced, belly up.

By now he was too far from the dock for me to reach him with the pole and noose. Without giving it another thought, I ran off the dock into the water and began to wade toward the big alligator with pole and noose in hand. I ended up in chest deep water by the time I got close enough to noose him. What happened next was a scene out of a nightmare. The big alligator rolled back over, belly down, and was directly facing me! I quickly angled backward toward the dock, telling Caleb to hand me the pistol I left lying on the dock. I positioned myself in the water to where I had a safe angle to take another shot.

I really had no idea what was going on. Was he still alive and had just been stunned? I was afraid, vulnerable, and didn't want to take any chances. He never moved after the second shot to the head, so I was able to get him noosed and pulled to shore. He measured twelve feet, two inches. I returned to the dock and was able to use the bang stick on the eight-foot alligator from there. I had to get back into the water to unwrap his rope which was tangled in the pilings. I was still a rookie in my first year as a nuisance trapper. If faced with the exact same scenario today, I would do everything differently. For one thing, I would absolutely not go face to face in the water with a twelve-foot alligator, even one I assumed to be dead (you know the old saying about when you assume!). I broke one of the Pappyisms 101: never go into the water with the gator. Experience is a great teacher.

The story behind the capture of my last twelve-foot alligator is pretty nondescript and dull compared to the stories behind the other captures. A large alligator had been terrorizing a neighborhood by walking through yards and across roads, moving from pond to pond. I set a trap using beef lung as bait. We use beef or pork lung whenever we set a bait. We get it from a local slaughterhouse. Everyone naturally assumes we use chicken. Beef or pork lung has a much stronger smell. It floats if the trap gets sprung whereas chicken sinks and the turtles and fish will eat it. It remains a viable bait for several days. We actually put it in a plastic bag and put it in the sun to ferment for a couple of days before we use it. You can smell it for miles and we always use gloves when we handle it. The smell will not wash off your bare hands for days. It's awful, but it's like cotton candy to an alligator.

By the time I returned to check the trap, it was well after dark. I saw he had taken the bait and was on the hook. The only thing unusual about this capture was that I was by myself in the dark. I brought my horse trailer and was able to back down to the water's edge, close to where I had set up the trap.

The alligator had already tired, having pulled against a hook for a while. I was able to noose him and also get a noose around his mouth so that I could safely tape it closed. I had rigged the horse trailer with a come-along winch to make getting him into the trailer easier. I secured the noose rope to the steel cable of the come-along and cranked the large alligator into the horse trailer without any real effort. I only had to lift his head over the back of the horse trailer about ten inches, and then the rest was like loading a boat onto a trailer. The alligator measured twelve feet, two inches and was still alive when I arrived at the processor's cooler. It was there that I euthanized him. The fact that I captured the alligator at night by myself is something I would never attempt to do today because of safety reasons. In both aforementioned stories, what I would do today is make every attempt to catch the alligators alive, keep them alive, and sell and release them alive to a licensed alligator farm.

The Program Director of SNAP called me one afternoon and asked me to respond to a call of an alligator bite on a golf course. A diver, who was retrieving golf balls in the ponds of one of Manatee County's nicer golf courses, had been bitten on the arm. It was a quick bite and release so the diver was going to be fine, but the alligator had to be removed. I called Kevin and asked him to assist me in catching it. Once the commotion from the emergency response crews settled down and normal play resumed, the alligator surfaced in the exact area the bite occurred. The alligator was very accustomed to seeing golfers passing by all day and was unfazed by us there.

It turned out to be an easy catch where Kevin hooked and I noosed the alligator. He was not big or aggressive, just an average six-foot gator that, until the bite, minded his own business. The very first thing that Kevin and I noticed was that the alligator was missing an eye on one side. We both concluded that the diver must have bumped into the alligator on his blind side. He could not see the diver in order to get out of the way. The bite was simply a defense mechanism to say, "Hey, I'm here, don't go bumping into me." Had the alligator wanted to attack, he could have grabbed the diver's arm and rolled. The diver could have lost his arm or maybe even his life.

I have been a certified diver since 1976. From what I have seen and experienced over the years as a diver and a trapper, there is no amount of money you could pay me to dive with alligators to retrieve golf balls. If the golf balls were any good, they would not have gone in the water in the first place!

Marcia and I are Tampa Bay Rays baseball fans and enjoy taking in a few games every year. One night we were fortunate enough to be given seats by friends that were immediately behind the Rays dugout. It was the closest we had ever been to the players and the action. It was in the fourth inning when I received a call from Kevin. He needed my help with an alligator he had hooked and had been fighting for over two hours in a neighborhood pond. The alligator was so large that it had been dragging him from backyard to backyard, and he was not able to get it close enough to shore to get a noose on it. The neighborhood was in a community near I-75 and I-275 and not too far from the stadium. We didn't hesitate to leave the game and those incredible seats.

Kevin and I have always been there for each other, and this night was no different. By the time we found Kevin, it was after 9:00 p.m. The first thing I did was get his keys and have Marcia take me to his truck which was parked several hundred yards away, where he had initially hooked the alligator. I was dressed in shorts, a Rays T-shirt and cap, and wearing my Sperry Docksiders. It was definitely not gatorin' apparel, but Marcia left me with Kevin anyway. I grabbed Kevin's backup rod from his truck and thankfully was able to find some bug spray in there as well.

I made my way back to Kevin and made a couple of casts toward the alligator. Fortunately, I was able to get another hook in the alligator, and eventually it began to run out of energy. Together we were able to drag the alligator close to shore. I held both rods, while Kevin got a noose on it, and together we were able to "1-2-3-pull, 1-2-3-pull" to get it out of the water.

Although we had permission to work anywhere around that large pond, it was a little unnerving walking through people's backyards at night. Most homeowners, however, never realized Kevin had been there fighting with the gator for hours. It seemed that no one noticed we were working on the large alligator, getting ready to drag it through an unsuspecting person's yard to the truck. As we were taping and securing the alligator, I suddenly had a flashlight pointed in my face. It was an elderly lady in a bathrobe wanting to know who we were and what in the hell we were doing there. Even though we explained what we were doing, she still demanded to see our identification.

"I need to see some credentials," she said.

We, of course, had our credentials with us and showed her, which seemed to make her happy. In all our years of trapping, this has been the only time Kevin or I have been asked for our credentials.

Once the alligator was out of the water and its mouth taped, Kevin had to make the thirty-minute drive to his house to pick up his 4-wheeler and trailer. My job was to sit on the bank in the darkness, hold the noose rope, and not let the alligator get back into the water. Kevin made it back an hour and fifteen minutes later. The 4-wheeler pulling the alligator to the road and into the trailer caused some lights to come on in the nearby houses. No one came outside, and the sheriff's office never showed up to see what was going on.

It was a smart move to get the 4-wheeler because Kevin and I could not have pulled the alligator that far. The alligator was a ten-foot-one-inch female. We were told that the Florida record for a female alligator was ten feet, two inches at that time. It was so close! This record was broken on October 10, 2019, by a female gator caught in my old hunting grounds at Lake George. The current state record for a female alligator is now ten feet, six and 5/8 inches. Female alligators seldom get above eight feet. The record for the largest male alligator is fourteen feet, three and a half inches. This alligator was caught in Lake Washington. The lifespan of alligators is thirty to fifty years, with some reaching seventy years.

I told the story earlier in the book about my great-grandfather, Robert, catching female alligators that were guarding their nests. Robert would tie them up while he and Pappy would collect the newborn hatchlings. He would then release the mama alligators in order to return the next year to do the same. I can tell you from personal experience that female alligators are extremely protective and fiercely guard their nests and their young. Mama alligators will issue a warning with a loud hiss. I suppose the hiss would be similar to a dog growling and baring its teeth. If you get too close, a mama alligator is probably going to lunge at you first. And if you dare to come closer...

One of my eCalls involved an alligator biting a riding lawn mower. The protective mama alligator totally caught the operator off guard. He fled the scene and could not go back to his lawn mower because the mama alligator refused to budge. It was as if she were now guarding the mower and holding it prisoner. The operator had accidentally come only a few feet from her nest. The mower was abandoned with its motor still running.

The operator didn't speak a word of English, and mi español es muy pobre (my Spanish is very poor). He did his best to tell me exactly what happened, and I just smiled saying, "Sí, sí (yes, yes)." Before I went to noose the mama gator, I spoke in Spanish to my new Mexican friend, "Ora por mí, por favor (pray for me, please.)" He actually managed a smile.

When I approached the mama alligator to noose her, she let me know in no uncertain terms that she was ready for a good fight. Throughout most of nature we observe mothers who are protective of their young. I have been attacked by small ducks that we call coots when I have accidentally gotten too close to their nests or their babies. This particular mama alligator was no longer than six and a half feet, but she fought me like a ten-foot bull alligator.

Did my great-grandfather, Robert, really subdue female alligators back in the 1920's, 1930's, and 1940's in order to collect their young? Or was this simply an alligator tale? Pappy swore it was true. I tend to believe Pappy because according to family legend, Robert Pappy was one tough old cracker who was not to be reckoned with. Robert was not afraid of any person or any alligator.

It makes me sad whenever I have to remove a female alligator from her nest. She is only doing what any mother would do. But a female alligator on a nest is definitely a threat to any person, pet, or lawn mower that gets too close. After I captured the mama alligator, securely taped her mouth and loaded her into the trailer, the Mexican man returned to his lawn mower. He had a big smile of relief on his face.

"Gracias, senior," he said. Sitting on his lawn mower he then said to me, "Dios te bendiga! (God bless you!)"

If the complainant asks for the nest to be removed, there is a procedure for doing so. The female must be captured first before SNAP will consider authorizing a nest removal. If approved, the trapper can then remove the eggs from the nest. There are several alligator farms in Florida that will gladly buy the eggs. The baby alligators will be raised in captivity until fully grown, when they will be butchered and their meat sold for human consumption. Their hides could be sold to companies like Gucci, Versace, Chanel, and J.B. Hill that specialize in alligator hide products such as purses, shoes, boots, wallets, and belts.

In 2003, I went to Captain's School and obtained my United States Coast Guard Captain's License (OUPV with training to 100 Ton Masters). While on a sabbatical leave, I did some inshore and offshore charters. Years later, I also did some guided hunts for people who obtained tags through the Statewide Alligator Harvest Program quota hunts. I met a local attorney when I removed a nuisance alligator for him. He had applied for and was chosen in the lottery for two tags for the Lake Manatee area. He asked me if I would serve as a guide. Although he had no experience with gatorin', he did well, and we had a great time. His first alligator measured over ten feet. It was definitely beginner's luck. We filled his second tag with a smaller seven-foot gator on a subsequent hunt. He could not have been happier. He showed up at my front door a few days later with a beautiful crossbow as a gift for me to express his appreciation.

A year later, I was contacted by a man who had recently retired at age fifty. Bill (not his real name) had moved to Florida after spending his career on Wall Street. He gave me the impression of a redneck wannabe. Bill had also applied for and received tags for Lake Manatee as his harvest area. He had no equipment, no boat, and no experience whatsoever. He seemed like a decent guy, and I agreed to take him gatorin'. I expected the hunt to go basically the same way as the hunt the year before with the attorney. Despite many similarities, it turned out quite different.

I met the man at the public boat ramp with my fourteen-foot aluminum boat with a 9.9 hp engine and all the equipment we would need. I became a little concerned when he showed up dressed like he was going to play golf.

The hunt began at sundown on a beautifully clear, still night. About an hour into the hunt, I shined some eyes that appeared to be a large alligator. I asked Bill if he wanted to try casting on the alligator and snagging it with a treble hook. He declined because he was afraid he might miss. I took the cast and immediately set the hook. The hooked alligator took off, but I reeled hard and soon we were on top of him. I brought the alligator alongside the boat and was able to get a breakaway dart in him like we use in "Run and Gun." The breakaway dart secured the alligator in case my hook came out. The dart also made it easier to get the alligator in a position to use the bang stick. I was able to pull the alligator to the surface next to the boat, and of course the alligator fought like crazy. Upon getting a glimpse of the size of the thrashing alligator, Bill asked me to cut the line.

"Are you kidding me?" I responded.

Bill said, "He is way too big. You're going to need a bigger boat (quoting the famous line from the movie, Jaws)."

It was then that I realized how scared this guy really was. I assured him that we were okay, and that I would euthanize the alligator soon (all alligators taken on public hunts must be euthanized as soon as possible).

It was understandable that he was scared. Here we are in a fourteen-foot aluminum boat in the middle of Lake Manatee in the dark with a hooked, darted, very large alligator thrashing against the gunwale of the boat. I somehow managed to hold on to the rope with the dart and I talked Bill into holding the rod with the hook still in the alligator.

"Just keep the line tight and don't pull," I told him. I would handle the rest.

I handed Bill some safety glasses, put my own glasses on, and loaded the bang stick with my free hand. Bill continued to suggest we abort this mission and simply cut the lines. Using only the light from my headlamp, I was able to very slowly get the alligator's head in perfect position about eight inches under the water. I pushed the bang stick against the kill zone, and there was a splash from the .44-mag bullet detonating. It was a perfect kill shot, and the alligator went limp.

Once I was absolutely sure the alligator was dead, I put a noose on the alligator's snout and pulled his head up over the gunwale, and taped his mouth closed. I did that for safety's sake and so we could get him back to the boat ramp without his mouth being open to take on water. I remember Bill squealing like a little girl as I was taping his mouth. Finally, Bill was able to relax.

I could tell that it would be impossible to load this alligator into the boat, so I had to secure him to the side of the boat and drag him slowly back to the ramp. I called Kevin and asked him to meet me at the ramp with his trailer. Bill also called his friend and asked him to meet us at the ramp.

The transformation of Bill over the next couple of hours was something to behold. Kevin and Bill's friend were waiting for us when we finally arrived. What was normally a ten-minute ride to the ramp took us over an hour because we were slowly dragging this large alligator tied to the side of our small boat. Once we were within voice range, Bill began hooting and hollering. Bill shouted to his friend, "You won't believe this alligator I just got!" Bill's account of what happened and what actually happened were very different. I didn't say a thing and let Bill have his moment. According to the account Bill gave to his friend, he had done everything, and I was just there to assist him.

The alligator measured eleven feet, six inches. It

took everything the four of us had to get this alligator in the trailer. Kevin and I asked Bill and his friend to follow us back to Kevin's house to help us transfer the alligator to Kevin's walk-in cooler. It was midnight when we finally got the alligator into the cooler.

Kevin, being the good guy he is, served a celebratory drink for everyone as we all listened to Bill recount his version of the night over and over again. For Bill and his friend, one drink turned into another, and neither one knew when it was time to go home. I left Kevin with Bill and his friend at 2:00 a.m., and they were still going strong. Kevin told me he went to bed at 4:00 a.m. and left Bill and his friend at the cooler still drinking. Who knows what time they finally left. I just hoped they would call their wives to come pick them up.

Bill had one more alligator tag and wanted to book another hunt with me. I told him how fortunate he had been to bag an eleven-foot-six-inch alligator on his first hunt. I told him that many people hunt all their lives and never see, much less get, an alligator that size. I agreed to another hunt, and Kevin and I took Bill and his friend out. We went in Kevin's War Eagle boat, using the trolling motor. Bill and his friend were perfectly content being spectators as I made a cast with the rod and reel and caught a very nice eight-foot-plus alligator which Kevin bang-sticked and taped. Kevin and I pulled the alligator into the boat as Bill and his friend watched. Bill and his friend were deeply disappointed that the hunt and season ended with such a "small" alligator. They were expecting another eleven-foot or larger alligator. Everyone I know would have been thrilled to bag an eight-foot alligator. We didn't invite them back to the cooler that night and I have never seen or heard from either one again. Kevin and I figure they are too busy catching thirteen-footers by themselves. They don't need us anymore.

CHAPTER SIX
Looking for Love in All the Wrong Places

If you have ever observed two alligators mating, doing the wild thing, making whoopee, or whatever you want to call it, you won't forget it. The male bellows loudly, and the lovemaking is very loud and very rough. Alligator mating season in Florida begins in early April and usually runs through late May. Female alligators normally build their nests and lay their eggs in late June. Incubation lasts 63-68 days, and hatching usually occurs in late August or early September. During mating season, males are on the move, looking for love.

While love is in the air, males tend to be more aggressive. I have personally removed alligators from front doors, garages, inside pool cages, in swimming pools, on roads and highways, in parking lots, in the middle of a soccer field during a game, and in fenced back yards. It seems that male alligators just lose their minds. To quote another song, "they will do anything for love!" Just watch the local news or scroll Instagram, and it seems the alligators are everywhere except in the water.

I remember responding to an early morning eCall. A young high school girl had just started driving and was heading out of the house to school. She got in her car and heard a loud hissing noise. She opened the door, and while holding onto the steering wheel, she leaned out and looked underneath her car. She came face to face with a seven-foot alligator. Of course she was freaked out, but she stayed in the car and called 911. The young lady and the alligator were waiting on me when I arrived.

I once got a 3:00 a.m. call from the Bradenton Police Department. An officer had discovered what he thought was a five-foot alligator under his car. I took my youngest son, Keyton, with me on the call. When we got there, we pulled an almost nine-foot-long gator from under the officer's car. When someone reports an alligator to be five to seven feet, it usually means the alligator is actually three to five feet long. An alligator reported to be eight to ten feet is more likely to be five to seven feet and a twelve-foot alligator is really a stocky nine-foot alligator. People usually overestimate and that is what we expect. Overestimation is not a problem. Underestimation can be a problem if you go on a call expecting to find a five-foot alligator and instead you find a ten-foot! Whenever I go on a call, I try to take the right equipment to handle whatever I happen to find.

I don't know what it is about alligators and front doors. Every year I seem to get six to eight calls of alligators at front doors. About half the time it is in the daytime and half the time it is at night. At night, people are usually awakened by a scratching sound or the dogs barking. Sometimes it is the Ring doorbell or the security camera going off. I have had people open the door in broad daylight only to be surprised by an unwelcome alligator.

I had a 3:00 a.m. eCall in the River Wilderness neighborhood a few years ago during the middle of mating season. I arrived to find a very distraught homeowner and two Manatee County sheriff deputies. There was a very large bull alligator that was looking for love and ended up at the front door. The homeowner was insisting that the deputies shoot the alligator. I noticed the home had beautiful double doors with very expensive leaded glass. The man said that if the alligator broke the glass and headed inside the house, he would shoot it. I knew there was a good chance that the leaded glass would be shattered whatever we did. I suggested we turn the lights off and stay back out of the way to see if the alligator would move away from the doors on his own. We waited for over an hour, and the alligator never budged.

I suggested plan B. I would back my truck up as close as I could to the front door and get a noose on the gator, but not tighten it. If tightened, he would begin rolling and thrashing, and the leaded glass would be history. If I could tie the rope to the hitch and allow the truck to jerk the alligator away from the doors quickly, it just might work. The alligator was so large that I wasn't sure I could have pulled him away from the front doors by myself anyway. I think Kevin was out of town, so I put in a call to the owner/farmer of the alligator farm that buys the gators I catch and asked him to help. He lived over an hour away. Finally, he arrived and agreed with the plan to use the truck. I kept plenty of slack in the rope and was slow and gentle when I got the noose around his neck. The plan was that I would slowly accelerate the truck to take the slack out of the rope, and then accelerate quickly to get the alligator away from the door and out onto the driveway. The plan worked perfectly, and the beautiful leaded glass doors were saved.

Taping his mouth shut was the next challenge. The alligator lunged at me and the farmer. There was no tree nearby to pull him against in order to steady him. I was eventually able to get a mouth snare around his jaws so his mouth was closed, but he was still lunging. The alligator was too big of a risk to jump on his back in order to pin him down. I had the sheriff deputies and the farmer hold the noose rope so the gator could not easily lunge forward, and I got his mouth taped shut. It took me, the farmer, the two deputies, and the homeowner to lift the alligator into the farmer's truck that had a covered, secure topper. The alligator measured eleven feet, six inches. It was daylight by the time the farmer pulled away with the alligator. I still have a sequence of pictures taken of this capture by onlookers. I think I remember this capture so well because later in the day we moved my mother into hospice care, but not before I gave her a detailed report of this capture.

My mother's Alzheimer's had progressed to the point that she had trouble responding. I am sure, though, that Dolores Pappy Rentz, who was instrumental in passing the gatorin' heritage on to me, was proud of me. During the last couple of years of her life, I would take her with me on certain permits so she could watch. I would set her up in a lawn chair. She always enjoyed going gatorin'. But on this day, I knew that this was the last gatorin' story I would share with the woman who had shared so many gatorin' stories with me. She passed on to life everlasting two days later.

Speaking of looking for love in all the wrong places, I have had a couple of situations that quickly became awkward. I once worked a permit where I had to make several trips to the location in an attempt to catch the alligator, which is not unusual. Every time I was there, the complainant and her husband were arguing, bickering, and talking ugly to each other. Both were cordial to me, but the amount and intensity of the arguing made me uncomfortable. I was glad to finally catch the alligator and not have to go back.

A few weeks after that, Marcia and I were on vacation. I got a call from the lady around 11:00 p.m. one night. She was slurring her words and sounded very inebriated. She told me that her husband was out of town for a few days and wondered if I could come over and "do some gator hunting, if you know what I mean." I think I knew what she meant, but I played stupid. After my initial shock, I told her that I was on vacation in the Keys with my wife and had other trappers on call for me in case of alligator-related emergencies. Then, I just stood there holding the phone in my hand, saying nothing. After a long pause, the lady said in a drunken slur, "Well... it was worth a try."

Twelve or thirteen years ago, Kevin and I went to check out a permit he had just gotten for a ten-foot alligator. After finding the location, we decided to first observe the pond from a distance in order to get an idea of how big this alligator really was. The complainant had a beautiful house and a well-manicured lawn with St. Augustine grass. We sat down in the grass to get a good vantage point of the spot where the alligator had been reported. The grass was soft but also a bit damp, like it had just been watered. Kevin and I sat there for about ten minutes when we noticed a lady walking toward us from the house across the street. We figured she was a neighbor who wanted to come advocate for the alligator and ask us why we were going to be taking it away.

Both Kevin and I noticed that she was a nice-looking, sharply dressed lady. She was wearing a very tight pair of white capri pants. I guessed she must have been in her early to mid-forties. She had a big smile on her face as she sat down on the damp grass right between Kevin and me. When she sat down between us, all I could think about was whether she'd ever get the grass stain out of the seat of those very white capri pants.

"Wow, you guys are the real thing! I can't believe it," she said. "I love you guys. Real alligator hunters. I have seen you on TV," she continued.

"No, that would not be us," we explained.

She continued heaping on the praise. "I saw your truck and trailer. You are the real deal. Alligator hunters… wow! Can I watch, please? I will be still and quiet, I promise. I've seen this alligator, and he is huge, like fifteen feet!" she continued.

Another thing that I immediately noticed about her was that she was one of those people who had the need to touch the person she was talking to. She was very touchy-feely. Kevin and I couldn't get a word in edgewise because she just kept talking and touching.

"Hey, where do you guys party?" she asked. That question made Kevin and me laugh.

"I really can't say that I have partied since I was in college, and that was a long time ago," I said.

"No… where do you guys go to hang out? My girlfriends and I go to this bar at St. Armands Circle. It is a cool place. You guys gotta come there, and I will introduce you to my girlfriends. Alligator hunters. They all will think you both are so cool…"

The jabber would not cease, and neither did the touching of our hands, arms, and shoulders. I figured this would be a good time to go ahead and play the first "M Card."

"Yeah, we really don't party or go to bars or clubs. We are just a couple of old married guys," I said, figuring that would be the end of this conversation.

But the opposite happened. The word "married" did not deter her, but rather seemed to motivate her to the next level.

"Hey, the alligator obviously is not here. Let's walk over to my house right now and have a drink," she offered.

Both Kevin and I protested, "We have to work…we have other calls to make…it's the middle of the afternoon…"

We were grasping at anything. Being gentlemen, we didn't want to be rude, but we both knew there was absolutely no way we were going to have a drink with her.

"Just one drink? Just one little drink? One drink

won't hurt." She was literally begging.

I was pretty sure that this lady was not accustomed to being turned down. I was just about to play the second "M Card — Minister" when she stood up and said, "I understand, you guys are busy right now, but please promise me you will come back later. That is my house right there, the little one. Don't come to the front door. I never use it. Come to the side because it's always open. You guys are welcome anytime and please come to St. Armands Circle and meet my girlfriends and come back here tonight when you get off work, just one drink?" she said in one never-ending sentence.

As she walked back to her house still smiling, waving good-bye for now and talking, I noticed the grass stain on the seat of those white capri pants. I asked Kevin, "Were we just propositioned, or was she on cocaine, or was she just overly friendly, or was she into alligator hunters, or are we just a couple of good looking, stud muffin, chick magnets, or... what just happened here?"

The next day, Kevin went back to see if the alligator ever showed up, and he took Julie with him. The alligator turned out to be a much smaller alligator and was captured. Neither Kevin or I ever went near that place again until this past year, when a permit I had took us by her house. As we drove by, I said to Kevin, "You reckon she ever got that grass stain out of those white capri pants?"

CHAPTER SEVEN
Close Calls

One of the questions that I get asked on most every call is, "Have you ever been bitten by an alligator?"

My answer is always, "No, not yet."

I am aware that it can happen at any time if you lose concentration or do something stupid. I have had a few close calls and done some stupid things, but I have been very fortunate. Recently, one of our trappers in another county almost lost his arm to a nine-foot alligator he was releasing at an alligator farm. When something like that happens, it really brings it home, and all of us become even more cautious.

On one of my very first eCalls, a large gator was seen crossing Tara Boulevard in Bradenton and was obstructing traffic by staying in the middle of the road. By the time I arrived, the alligator had moved into someone's backyard and was in a hedge next to their pool cage. I walked up to check things out and was surprised when the alligator lunged and then charged me. He came toward me only about six feet before stopping, but I was completely unprepared. Had he wanted to continue his charge, he could have easily grabbed me.

Alligators can move extremely fast on land. I believe that the alligator realized he was cornered and was just establishing his ground. I had a similar situation a few years after that. It was a 2:00 a.m. eCall for an alligator at the entrance of a neighborhood off Lockwood Ridge Road. A female sheriff's deputy was on the scene and held her flashlight on the alligator as I approached him with my noose and noose pole. When I got close, the alligator turned and charged directly at me. My truck was close by, and I literally jumped up on my back bumper. When I turned around, I realized that the alligator had only charged a few feet, but it was enough to get me moving out of his path. The deputy asked me if I wanted her to shoot the alligator, and I told her no, absolutely not! I regrouped and noosed the alligator, and it turned out to be an easy catch.

Out of the hundreds of alligators I have caught, what made these two alligators charge? I think it was because they felt cornered. Of course, most of the other alligators I have caught on land were also cornered with no place to go, but they did not charge me. I have no answer as to why these two did, but it taught me to always be ready for the unexpected. And don't ever paint yourself into a corner where you can't escape if they should charge.

Other close calls were simply my own stupidity. Like the time I had set a bait on a pond, and the pond was surrounded by a steep slope. I went to check the bait at first daylight, and the alligator was hooked but lying on the bank with his mouth open. Instead of walking at an angle down the slope, I took a more direct route. My rubber boots slipped on the wet grass, and I quickly found myself sliding toward the alligator. At least I had the presence of mind to roll onto my belly and grab the grass and ground to stop the slide. I have been very much aware of steep banks from then on.

One time I had a 4:00 a.m. eCall in my own neighborhood where a five-foot alligator was at a neighbor's front door. It was a cool morning, and the alligator was unusually docile, maybe because of the cooler temperature. It was an easy catch. I taped his mouth shut but didn't bother to tape his legs for the two-minute ride back to my house, where I would transfer him to the trailer. I did leave the noose on him and tied the rope to a cleat in the truck, just in case. By not taking the time to tape his legs, unbeknownst to me, he had crawled out of the back of the truck, and I had been dragging him along the asphalt road.

As I made the turn to my house 300 yards away, I noticed that he had climbed out. I stopped the truck, reached down in the darkness to pick him up, then suddenly noticed that his mouth was open. It had only taken a few seconds for the asphalt to disintegrate the electrical tape holding his mouth closed. If I had grabbed him, he would have undoubtedly chomped my hand. Stupid. I have never made that mistake again.

I once had a permit for a very large alligator that was eating a farmer's calves. The farmer had several ponds on his remote property. He swore that the alligator was at least eighteen feet long. The gate to the property was locked with a combination lock, so the farmer gave me the combination to come and go as I pleased. I had a bait set on one of the secluded ponds where calves had gone missing.

One evening, about an hour before dark, I went to check the bait. The bait was gone, and there was nothing on the line, so I decided to reset it. The rope had become entangled, and to untangle it I had to wade out into the pond a couple of feet. I had water boots on and took a step into the black pond water, and I stepped directly on the back of what I estimated to be a six-foot alligator. I am not sure who was more startled, the alligator or me. Neither one of us could have moved in the opposite direction any faster. I am pretty sure that I needed to change my underwear. I also thought, "Nobody even knows I am here." If something had happened, no one would even have any idea where to start looking for me. STUPID!

Probably the closest I have come to what could have been a bad bite was for an eCall with an eight-foot-four-inch alligator that had gotten into a fenced backyard. I easily noosed him and was able to drag him to a tree and get him secured tightly so I could tape his mouth. I thought I had him tight enough to get on his back, pin his head, and tape his mouth. I didn't realize that he still had room to roll. I was on top of him with his head pinned to the ground, getting ready to tape his mouth, when he rolled to his right and in doing so, threw me off of him. His mouth came open, and thankfully the noose was tight enough against the tree so that he could not reach me. STUPID, STUPID, STUPID! Now, whenever I am working alone, I just secure the mouth with a mouth snare. It doesn't look as cool to the people watching, but it is so much safer.

All of these instances happened more than ten years ago. I learned from my mistakes. Again, experience is a good teacher. I am much, much more careful now that I am older and wiser. Gatorin' involves a certain amount of risk, and you can never be too cautious. Just three months ago, I went on a permit where I caught an alligator less than four feet long. I taped his mouth and carried him up to my truck and trailer. I had the trailer locked, so I slipped a snare around his neck and tied him to the trailer to keep him from running away while I unlocked the trailer and gathered up my equipment. Once the trailer was unlocked, I slipped the snare off the alligator, dropped the snare on the ground, and walked to the front of the trailer. I didn't notice that I had stepped into the snare until a step later, when I fell flat on my face; I dropped the alligator and got caught in my own snare.

I gazed back at the complainant's house and noticed that the entire family was watching me through the window. I know I must have looked like a total moron or a circus clown. The alligator could have run away while I was getting my foot out of the snare. Thankfully, he didn't move. I guess he must have enjoyed a laugh, too. A young man came out to check on me and ask if I was OK. My response was, "Well, I have never done that before." Another lesson learned.

CHAPTER EIGHT
Patty

This chapter really does not belong in this book. This chapter is not about alligators, but rather about a dog. It happened in May of 2012. I was coming home from an alligator call, and it was close to midnight. At that time, we lived about twelve miles out of town on a five-acre lot in a country subdivision called Foxbrook. I was on a dark, uninhabited stretch of road and noticed some kind of animal sitting on the white line on the passenger side of the road. Just as I passed, the animal turned and looked into my approaching headlights. I had absolutely no idea what kind of animal it was. Honestly, it looked to me like a tiny koala bear. I turned the truck around to investigate.

It was a very small and old Boston Terrier. I spoke gently to her and petted her on the head before picking her up. Her eyes were milky white, and apparently covered with cataracts. I wondered how in the world she had gotten there. There were no houses nearby, and there was no traffic that night on that stretch of road. For some unknown reason, I had a crate for a small dog in the truck so I put her in it. She never whined, whimpered, or cried. When I got home, I gave her something to eat, some water, and left her in the crate in the garage because I wasn't sure how our three Labrador retrievers and two golden retrievers would receive her. I also wanted to give her a bath before bringing her inside.

Marcia was sound asleep, so I didn't mention anything to her about the dog until 4:30 a.m. when Marcia got up for work. I told her I found a dog on the way home and she was in the garage.

"WE ARE NOT GOING TO KEEP HER!" she said.

When I got up, I took the dog to our veterinarian to scan for a chip. There wasn't one. I spent the day checking neighborhoods that were closest to where I had found her to see if there were any lost dog signs. I checked with animal control to see if anyone was looking for a lost dog. I couldn't find anything that indicated someone had lost a dog. I gave her a bath, and that evening I introduced her to our family and the other dogs. Everyone welcomed her. She immediately began to bond with me. I thought that someone would report her lost. But apparently, someone must have just dumped her. How she didn't get run over, eaten by a coyote or even an alligator, or get lost in the woods was a miracle.

Marcia told me I needed to find her a home because we already had enough dogs. I knew one way that I would be able to keep her: if I could get Alaina to cry and beg her mother to let us keep the dog. I knew Marcia would never tell Alaina no. Alaina and I schemed, and it worked. Marcia gave in, and Alaina named her Patty. Patty became a member of our family.

The veterinarian guessed that little Patty was between thirteen and fifteen years old. She was found with a collar, which she wore the rest of her life. She was blind, deaf, and had some very bad teeth which had to be removed. One of her eyes became infected a few months after she came to live with us, and we had it removed. Despite her bad sight and hearing, she must have had an incredible sense of smell because she always knew where I was.

She was constantly at my feet or in my lap. She loved to paw me and beg for food whenever we were at the dinner table. If we were watching TV, she would be in my lap. If I was in my office, she would find me and sit on my feet. My office and our bedroom were upstairs, and Patty quickly learned to count and navigate the stairs without an issue. The only exception was when she occasionally miscounted on the way down and jumped before she got to the last step.

I always wrote my sermons at the dining room table and Patty always sat on my feet as I wrote. I always knelt and still kneel beside my bed at night to say my evening prayers. Patty lay on top of my outstretched legs as I prayed. She slept on a pet bed in front of my nightstand, getting as close to me as she could. When Marcia got up early to get ready for work, I would reach down and put Patty in bed next to me where she would snuggle. She loved to get under the covers. When we were outside going for a walk, she followed me and seemed to know exactly where I was.

I came to love this little dog more than any dog I had ever had. And I truly had loved all my dogs from childhood on. We have always had retrievers, and we have done field trials and hunt tests. Patty could not retrieve or hunt or even swim. She fell into the pool a couple of times, and she hated the water. She was not a working dog, she was the very first and only small dog I ever had. Patty really could not do much of anything. Why did I love this particular dog so much? Maybe it was because I had rescued Patty. Maybe it was because Patty was old, and I knew I would not have her very long. Maybe it was a combination of those two things. And maybe, in some way, she had also rescued me at the same time. My brother said to me on several occasions that Patty had changed my life. She did. Through Patty, I was able to see and understand some things in ways I never thought about before. Patty also helped me better understand some things about God.

I held her and used her as a sermon illustration during the Christmas Eve candlelight services in my last year at Emmanuel United Methodist Church in Bradenton and my first year at Sun City Center United Methodist Church. As I held Patty, I shared how I had rescued her and how much I loved her. I then talked about how God sent his Son, Jesus, to rescue us and how much God loves us.

Despite her age and her obvious issues, Patty lived a great life and was pretty spoiled. She stayed active until the last couple of weeks of her life, when she began having seizures for the first time. She also lost weight because she didn't want to eat. I knew the time had come to make that horrible decision to not let her suffer. I made an appointment with our veterinarian, who had taken such good care of her over the two years and ten months we shared her life.

As happens with many humans, Patty rallied the night before the appointment and was active and playful and her old self for a couple of hours. But the next day, I had no doubt that I had made the right decision. I didn't know it was possible to love a little dog as much as I loved Patty. I held her and wept as Dr. Gartenberg administered the euthanasia.

I include this reflection about Patty because it was an after-hours alligator call that caused me to be on that road the night I found her. Otherwise, I would never have been on that particular road at that time of night. I am convinced that God uses and maybe even designs instances like me finding Patty. As I reflect on my life, it is in the God-designed moments that we get a glimpse of what our lives are all about, and what life itself is all about. How truly fortunate we are, when we allow God to mold and shape our lives, teaching us the depths of His amazing love for us.

CHAPTER NINE
Living in Wild Kingdom

I grew up watching Marlin Perkins and Mutual of Omaha's Wild Kingdom, which aired from 1963 to 1985. Living in Florida is somewhat akin to living in a "Wild Kingdom." We have alligators that just walk around and show up everywhere. We have huge pythons and all kinds of poisonous and non-poisonous snakes. We have crocodiles, iguanas, panthers, bears, and sharks. We have some people who love the "Wild Kingdom" in which we live, and we have those who don't love anything about the natural wildlife that is unique to our Floridian culture.

    I suppose the thing I never realized until becoming a nuisance alligator trapper was that I would either be absolutely hated or absolutely loved by half the population of Florida. Some perceived me, the alligator trapper, as an awful person who took great pleasure in upsetting the balance of nature and killing God's innocent creatures. I have been screamed at, cussed out, and physically threatened for simply doing my job. I have set traps which were either stolen, destroyed, or thrown into the pond. I remember one couple who, when I showed up to cover a permit, started banging pots and pans to scare away alligators that they were in fact feeding. These fed alligators had become a serious threat to the pets and small children who lived next door.

A trapper who worked in Manatee County before I was hired told me the story about one guy he encountered while doing his job. The trapper had an alligator on the line, and this guy walked up to him with a knife drawn, threatening the trapper. The guy then proceeded to cut his line. The trapper contacted the sheriff's office, and the man was arrested and charged with assault with a deadly weapon. The trapper truly thought the guy was coming after him! A year after this incident and this man's arrest, while working a permit on the same pond, I also had an encounter with the guy. He cursed me and threatened me from his back yard. Some people are either crazy, or they just never learn. It is sad when the people become more dangerous than the alligator.

Recently, I was issued a permit to remove a nine-foot alligator from a neighborhood pond. This alligator had begun to wander through the neighborhood and to rest up against pool cages, especially those with dogs. As I stood surveying the pond, I suddenly had a woman in my face. I had been warned about her by at least a dozen neighbors. One neighbor, who was flying a Trump flag in front of his house, pointed out the Prius in her driveway with the Harris/Walz bumper sticker. Clearly, the toxicity existed in this neighborhood long before I arrived, and it really had nothing to do with alligators. She was already out of control, yelling at me. I attempted to be polite as I asked her to get out of my personal space.

"I am going to call the cops and have you arrested for taking an alligator out of its natural habitat," she screamed as her spittle hit me in the face."

"Please make the call to the sheriff's office, because if you don't, I will," I said. "Here is the number. I have it on speed dial. You will be the one arrested for impeding me from doing my job. You have to understand that it is your home and all of these new homes and subdivisions that have removed these alligators from their natural habitats," I reasoned.

She used some choice four-letter words and flipped me off with both hands while retreating to her house.

When someone is that passionate and that angry, you just hope that they do not own a gun. Florida Fish and Wildlife Conservation Commission (FWC) officers and local law enforcement have no tolerance for people who act like that. Thankfully, that extreme type of behavior is not the norm. Many people just enjoy seeing the alligators and argue that the alligator is not hurting a thing. We are not there to hunt down alligators who are minding their own business.

People get really torqued because nuisance alligators are euthanized. According to the most recent statistics I could find, around eight thousand nuisance alligators are euthanized every year. There are approximately 3.1 million alligators in the state of Florida. That would mean that

0.62% of the total gator population is euthanized every year for being a nuisance.

On average, another 6 to 8.5 thousand alligators are euthanized each year as a result of the Statewide Alligator Harvest Program public quota hunts, according to the statistics from the last ten years. If there was any danger or threat whatsoever to the alligator population in Florida, the public quota hunts would not exist. What I am saying is that there is no shortage of alligators. If anything, there may even be an overabundance. But I agree with the argument: they were here first, and they deserve to be here!

I have mellowed a lot in my old age. I don't do the public alligator hunts anymore. I have become much more of a "live and let live" person now when it comes to hunting most anything. For many years, I was an avid deer hunter. Not so much anymore. I have no need to kill an animal for the sake of killing (except when it comes to armadillos, coyotes, or wild hogs). An armadillo or wild hog can destroy a lawn and landscape overnight and a coyote can and will kill your pets.

When it comes to the alligators I catch, I much prefer to catch them alive and sell them live to licensed alligator farms. I have been doing this for years. That way, euthanization is out of my hands, and I make more money. I do occasionally take an alligator to the processor, or Kevin and I will process an alligator for the meat. Again, prepared and cooked correctly, alligator meat is really good to eat. Every nuisance alligator trapper I know in the state of Florida, when they euthanize the alligator, process or have the alligator processed for human consumption. Alligators are not just killed for the sake of killing and taken to the dump.

As Florida continues to quickly develop more and more communities, more and more alligators will come into contact with humans. Every year I seem to get more and more eCalls to remove alligators from public places. Occasionally, you hear of a tragic bite or death as a result of an alligator attack. Sadly, I predict that we will see more and more human/pet alligator incidents as the new developments continue to be built.

Remaining calm and trying to reason didn't work with the crazed, angry lady in the last story. However, I have found that talking to people in a calm, reasonable voice and explaining why you are doing what you are doing goes a long way. While they might not agree, most people are at least respectful.

On the other hand, some people do not want to see or ever have to deal with any alligator. They just want the alligator gone, and they really don't give a rip what happens to it. So, for many people, I am a hero. I have had many people hug me and cry while thanking me for capturing and removing the alligator. Still, there are others who enjoy seeing the alligators until they lose a pet to the alligator, or the alligator shows up in their pool, garage, or at the front door.

I was on a call recently for a ten-foot-seven-inch alligator in a pool. It was discovered that the alligator had punched out screens on each end of the lanai, and for several nights, had been using that lanai as its own private superhighway to travel between ponds, taking the shortest and most direct route. The homeowner discovered the broken screens and noticed that the lanai furniture had been rearranged every night for several nights. He thought it was a raccoon, until one night the alligator decided to stay in the pool. Kevin was issued the permit, and together we safely removed the alligator.

The following two stories are just a couple of the many reasons why I am a nuisance alligator trapper. It's really not about the alligators as much as it is about the people.

In my early days of being a nuisance trapper, I was issued a permit in the most rural part of Manatee County. The complainant was a cattle farmer, who I could describe as one of the last living, true-to-life Florida crackers. Large alligators were killing and eating his calves. It was a twenty-five-mile drive one way to his farm from where I lived, but I never minded the drive. The only way I can describe it is that I felt like I was going back to my grandfather's farm.

Mr. Jake reminded me so much of Pappy, and he made me feel like a kid again. It was like a slice of heaven to just be out in the pasture around the cows. It was wonderful to hang out with Mr. Jake, who stood there in his cowboy hat and boots, telling story after story. If he knew I was coming out, his wife, Mrs. Becky, would cook up a farm fresh meal, and I was invited to dinner. The meals were amazing!

Most trips to Mr. Jake's farm were never quick ones. Sometimes I stood at the truck, listening to him tell stories about his childhood and his ancestors until it was time for him to go to bed. Life on a cattle ranch begins early. Of course, his stories were different from the stories Pappy told, but they were from a similar genre. It was always wonderful to listen to and learn from Mr. Jake. I had a hide tanned from an alligator caught on his property and gave it to him. He sent the hide to a place in Texas that fashioned a custom pair of cowboy boots for him. I am sad to say that I allowed myself to get so busy that I had not been out to see him in several years. It was my plan to surprise him and to present him with a copy of this book. I was saddened to learn that he passed on to everlasting life earlier this year. Mr. Jake was a blessing to me and to everyone who knew him.

In 2015, I received a permit for a twelve-foot alligator that had gone into a backyard of an upscale golf community and attacked and killed a dog. I learned from the complainant over the phone that there were small children present with the dog when this happened. When I arrived on scene, I found an alligator that was at least twelve feet long in the middle of the pond behind the residence. At the end of the pond was an eight-foot alligator swimming with what appeared to be the remains of the dog in his mouth. Several people who had witnessed the attack on the dog were present when I arrived, and all were certain that it was the large alligator, not the eight-footer, that was responsible for the death of the dog. The bigger alligator was not within casting range, and I would definitely need help with him later.

In the meantime, the smaller alligator had let go of the remains of the dog, and I was able to cast and retrieve them. I put the remains in a contractor-sized garbage bag, which I always carry in my truck. I called and asked the complainant if he wanted the remains or if he would like me to have them cremated. If so, I offered to cover the cost and get them back to him. I also volunteered to bury the remains on our six-acre property, under a tree in our pasture. He preferred that I just bury the remains.

Before I left, I was able to snag and remove the eight-foot alligator which turned out to be a female. When I got to my house, I buried this beloved dog whose name was Bear. I said prayers, thanking God for Bear and asking for comfort for his family, especially the young girls who would never forget the trauma of watching their pet get killed and dragged away. I thanked God for protecting the children. Everyone there knew that the alligator could have easily grabbed one of the children instead of Bear.

I went back later that afternoon to the golf course community and was able to meet the complainant, David, and his beautiful family. He, like Marcia, was a physician, and was so appreciative of all that I had done. The large alligator was still in the pond, and I called Kevin to see if he could help me. Kevin was tied up with another alligator call in west Bradenton. He said he would send his wife, Julie, to help me and he would get there as soon as he could. I was able to get a hook set in the beast. An hour later when Julie arrived, she also got a hook in the alligator, who then proceeded to pull us from backyard to backyard around the pond. Kevin arrived after it was dark, and he also got a hook in the gator.

Even with our three hooks in him, we were not able to get him close enough to the bank to get him noosed. I had been fighting him for three hours, Julie for two hours, and Kevin for an hour when the alligator finally decided he had had enough. With a burst of strength, he took off across the pond, breaking all of our 100-pound test Power Pro lines in the process. I have never before or since experienced an alligator that strong. That alligator was never seen again in that pond or anywhere in that area that I am aware of after that night. It was incredibly frustrating to me that we were not able to capture the alligator responsible for killing the dog, Bear.

I have often wondered if that alligator is still living somewhere in a swamp. David had a metal fence installed around the property. While a fence will not keep alligators out, it will at least slow them down or hopefully deter them so they move along.

I saw David several times over the next few years when I was working permits in his community. I would always stop and visit with him for a few minutes if he was outside working in the yard. In 2019, almost five years after the incident with Bear, David called me one evening to tell me their other dog, Pearl, had died of old age. He asked me if I could take her and bury her next to Bear.

"Of course," I said.

I went to pick her up and had the opportunity to sit with David on his lanai as he and his wife and children said their goodbyes to Pearl. That night, David recounted the incident with Bear, saying that Bear was protecting the children and gave his life to keep the alligator from attacking them. I absolutely believe that is exactly what happened. David asked me if I would say a prayer with him and his family before I left. I remember thanking God again for Bear and for Pearl and for the gift of these wonderful animals that enrich our lives. David thanked me, gave me a big (Bear) hug, and thanked me again before I left.

We have continued to loosely stay in touch with David and his family. I once had to stay overnight in the hospital that David works at. When he found out I was there, he came to my room and visited me. Over the years, Marcia and I have received beautiful Christmas cards from David that show his children growing up. Although we don't see each other or really talk anymore, I believe I have a deep connection with David and his family. I believe I could pick up the phone, and if I needed anything, he would be there. If he called me, I would do the same for him.

Whenever I encounter those very few people who curse and scream when I am simply doing my job, I choose to remember and think about David and his family, about Mr. Jake, and about so many of the other amazing, wonderful people I have had the opportunity to meet as a nuisance trapper. I wouldn't trade these experiences for anything.

CHAPTER TEN
Study Hard, Bubby

Eight years ago, I received a permit for a seven-foot alligator in a new housing development off Rye Road. The complainant's house and one other house across the street from his were some of the very few homes that were completed in the neighborhood. He was a friendly, outgoing man who had recently made the move to Florida from his native Minnesota. The pond behind his house offered a beautiful setting that backed up to a preserve. It was one of those gorgeous, natural ponds that would attract an alligator with all its cover. That area would not be developed, and he would always have a great view from his backyard.

He had encountered his first alligator when it showed a very special interest in the man's dog. Because of the wooded preserve behind his house, I explained that once we remove this alligator, another would probably take its place very soon. As I was preparing to catch and remove the alligator, he explained that a single mom from New

Jersey and her eleven-year-old son, Bobby, had moved into the house across the street recently. Bobby had an interest in alligators, and the man asked if Bobby and his mother could come over to observe the capture.

"Of course," I responded.

The man called his new neighbor on his cell phone and invited her and Bobby to come watch. Bobby came running across the street with a big smile on his face. His mother, still dressed in business suit attire, shook my hand, introduced herself, and told me her name (which I don't remember). And with her thick New Jersey accent she called her son BUBBY, instead of Bobby.

I spent some extra time with Bubby showing him the equipment I would be using and explaining to him how I would catch the alligator. Meanwhile, Bubby's mom complained about the heat and the bugs, and she sarcastically teased, "And on top of the bugs and the hot weather and the hurricanes, now I am going to have to deal with alligators. How could I have ever left the shores of Jersey (pronounced Joursezy) to live in this jungle?" she said several times loudly in her very strong New Jersey accent. I sensed that she was only half-teasing.

Bubby was beside himself with excitement and anticipation. I put on a gatorin' clinic that was truly flawless. I was able to call the alligator to me, make a perfect cast on the first try, set the treble hook, and tire out the alligator, which was making the drag scream each time he made a run. I brought him to shore and was able to hold the rod with one hand as I slipped the noose around his neck with the other hand. I then pulled the alligator up the bank and secured him to a tree, where I got on his back, pinned his head, and taped his mouth.

I pulled the alligator to the truck, picked him up, and invited Bubby to stand next to me while his mom took a few pictures. The smile never left Bubby's face. I put the alligator in the trailer and was gathering my equipment when Bubby's mother, who had actually been unusually quiet during the capture, said to him, "Bubby, this is exactly why I tell you to study hard and do well in school and get a good education, so that when you grow up, you won't have to do a job like this."

"WHAT??" I thought to myself. Did she really just go there? I do not get offended easily, but she went way over the line. Maybe it was just a New Jersey thing to bust my chops, but she surely didn't know me well enough to do that. I consider myself to be a "southern gentleman."

At first I thought I should not respond, so that I wouldn't say something I would later regret, but there was no way I could let this go. I looked directly at Bubby and said to him, "Bubby, you can study hard, do well in school, get a good education, and still do this."

Then I looked at Bubby's mom and said, "I have a bachelor's degree from Florida Southern College, a master's degree from Emory University, and I earned my doctorate at Boston University. I also did post-doctoral work in the field of mental health counseling at Florida Gulf Coast University. Before I leave, I will give you a website, and you can check my credentials. I do this job not because I have to, but because I love doing it. For me, it's a family thing. My ancestors were alligator trappers, and it is in my blood."

Bubby's mom looked a bit shocked and began to apologize. I honestly don't believe she realized how offensive her comment was. What if I had zero education and still did this job? No one should be put down because of their job.

My father, Charlie Rentz, was a farmer. He dropped out of school after the fourth grade to work on the farm. Both of his parents died young, and he promised his father on his deathbed that he would raise his younger brothers and sisters—a promise he fulfilled. Dad was the oldest surviving child in his family. After Pearl Harbor was bombed, Dad enlisted in the U.S. Army Air Corps and served his country faithfully throughout World War II. After the war was over, he left the farm and went to work in the Pappy Products jelly factory in Jacksonville. He eventually married the boss's daughter, Dolores Pappy.

My dad was the hardest-working person I have ever known and was very successful. However, he was always self-conscious about his lack of an education, and he wanted me and my brother to get a good education. My father was the driving force behind me earning my doctorate, even though he never lived to see it. Moreover, he wanted us to do something we loved.

I loved and was passionate about the thirty-nine years I spent in ministry. I have also absolutely loved being an alligator trapper, especially now in my retirement. It helps to keep me healthy and in shape because it is rigorous to work outside in the heat of a Florida summer. If you don't believe me, try removing an almost eleven-foot, 450-pound alligator from a swimming pool and put him in a trailer when he would rather be in a pond.

EPILOGUE

It is my understanding that 26,000 Minorcan descendents now reside in St. Johns County and the St. Augustine area. Minorcan cultural events take place in St. Augustine throughout the year. Minorcan food such as Minorcan clam chowder, fromajardis (cheese pastries), and pilau (seasoned rice) are on the menu in some of the restaurants. A number of the restaurants even serve alligator meat!

    Pappy's Seafood in St. Augustine, which closed back in the 1980's, was owned by some of our relatives. It was the place to go out to eat in the 60's and 70's. I found some pictures of the old restaurant on Facebook. It was definitely my family's favorite restaurant. I remember going there numerous times when I was growing up.

    I have often thought and even dreamed about the idea of opening a new Pappy's Seafood Restaurant in St. Augustine with a Minorcan menu. It would feature Gaspar Papi's fried alligator, Ana Pons Papi's alligator stew, Jose

Vitorio Papi's smoked alligator, Robert Pappy's alligator gumbo seasoned with datil pepper, Gerald Pappy's grilled alligator and rattlesnake skewers, and Dolores Pappy Rentz's fromajardis! Sounds like a great business venture to me! If only I had the financial resources. But where would I find the time?

If you have made it this far in the book, I am sure that you have wondered how I faithfully served as the senior pastor to a large congregation with a paid staff of thirty people and still found time to be a nuisance alligator trapper? Over the years, I became very adept at time management. I kept regular on campus office hours. Fortunately, I had several associate pastors on staff who helped share the pastoral ministry. I spent a lot of time team/staff-building, working with my amazing staff, and delegating responsibility.

For eight years of my ministry at Sun City, I was blessed with Pastor Sam as my senior associate pastor. Sam took care of the daily operation of the church. By having several associate pastors and a strong staff, it freed me up to do what I did best which was to cast the vision, preach, and lead worship. My general work week at church was never less than forty-five hours. It was a very busy place. Before Covid, we were having six worship services every weekend. This number dropped to four after Covid. I never mentioned trapping alligators to the congregation, and I would bet that 98% of the congregation didn't even know I was a nuisance alligator trapper.

So when did I have time to run permits and catch alligators? My days off were Friday and Saturday, so those days were dedicated to gatorin'. Sometimes I worked permits right after sunrise and just before dark. Obviously, I could not begin to keep up with all of my permits. Robert, Kevin, and designated agents Brandon, Jimmy, and Cameron covered permits and eCalls that I was not able to cover. I kept up with all of my paperwork and monthly report forms. None of my permits were ever missed.

These guys truly covered for me, did a superb job, and "kept me in the game" until I retired. There was something very therapeutic for me to go gatorin' during those very busy times before I retired. Gatorin' was, and still is, my happy place where I can forget about the stresses of life for a while.

One question I get asked now is, "When will you give up gatorin'?" I suppose I get asked that question because I look so old now. My answer is always, "I plan to continue gatorin' as long as I am physically able to safely catch alligators."

Pappy knew when it was time to walk away, and I am confident that I will know, too. I recognize that I am not as strong or as quick as I once was, but I am much wiser and way more careful now than ever before. I hope, pray, and plan to continue for several more years. I will turn seventy on March 23, 2026. I am hoping to get a permit and catch an alligator on my 70th birthday! Right now, I am finally learning to take life a day at a time.

All of my sons, Caleb, Cody, Keyton, and Josh, assisted me while they were growing up. All are skilled and adept in catching an alligator. Each one has stories to tell about their favorite gatorin' adventure. One big reason for writing this book is so that they and others will have our family history and my stories recorded to share with future generations. I think Cody is probably the one who loves gatorin' the most. I have not run across anyone who is able to cast as far and as accurately as he does. I suspect that at least one of the boys, maybe even all of them, will continue in the footsteps of Gaspar, Jose Vitorio, Joseph, Robert, Gerald (Pappy), Dolores, and now me. Gatorin'! It is in our blood, and it is definitely a family tradition!

PICTURE INDEX

1. Me holding a small alligator I caught by the tail with my brother Bob. I believe I was around nine years old at the time, and Bob was four years younger.
2. Robert Pappy (1879-1945), my great-grandfather and the man responsible for coining the word "gatorin."
3. My grandfather, Pappy, and his beloved Nellie. I could not find a picture of him with an alligator.
4. A plaque in St. Augustine commemorating the oldest Roman Catholic parish in the United States where my great-great-great-aunt, Josefa, was the first child baptized.
5. Me standing outside of the 'Don Toledo"/Gaspar (Papi) Papy House in St. Augustine.
6. A plaque commemorating the "Don Toledo"/Gaspar Papy house.
7. My mother, Dolores Pappy Rentz. I wasn't able to find a picture of her with an alligator either. She was always the one taking the pictures when we were children.
8. A recent picture of me with a sixteen-inch alligator I removed from a lanai.
9. A gator I caught during the "Run and Gun" days.
10. Kevin and me.
11. Me around age twelve with an alligator I caught in a net. It was a definite "catch and release."
12. A plaque in St. Augustine commemorating the Minorcan heritage.
13. Me with a big ten-foot gator I caught and put in the trailer by myself.

14. Airboat driver, James, with my twelve-foot-three-inch Istokpoga alligator.
15. My son, Josh, who is now thirty two years old, when he was much younger.
16. My youngest son, Keyton, who is now twenty-eight years old, when he was much younger.
17. Me with my sister-in-law, Shelli, and an eight-foot alligator.
18. Me with an eleven-foot eCall alligator I removed from a front door.
19. Olin's backyard during "Run and Gun" season.
20. Kevin and me
21. My oldest son, Caleb, with a nine-foot alligator.
22. My wife, Marcia, with her eleven-foot alligator.
23. Patty
24. An eleven-foot alligator I removed from a golf course pond.
25. My second oldest son, Cody, with a nine-foot alligator he snagged and caught while I watched.
26. A ten-foot alligator that required Robert and the winch on his truck.
27. A nine-foot gator that decided to walk across a soccer field during a game.
28. An eleven-foot alligator I snagged late one afternoon. Kevin came to assist me. It was well after dark when we finally got him taped and in the trailer.
29. A ten-foot alligator from a guided hunt that I led.

THE MINORCAN HERITAGE

The Minorcans, some 1,300 people of Mediterranean origins, were brought to Florida in 1768 as contract employees to farm a large indigo plantation at New Smyrna, 70 miles south of St. Augustine. Though most came from the island of Minorca off the eastern coast of Spain, their number included others from Greece, Sicily and Italy.

Death and hardship became their lot and after nine years they abandoned the New Smyrna community. Granted sanctuary by British authorities in St. Augustine, those able walked the long, weary miles northward in the hot summer of 1777.

Here they settled on land south of the Castillo de San Marcos. Some engaged themselves as tradesmen, others took up farming and many fished in the bountiful ocean waters. This area became home to generations of Minorcans to follow.

When Spain regained Florida in 1784, the Minorcans cast their fortunes with the new regime and stayed in St. Augustine when Florida joined the United States in 1821. Gradually they lost their native languages, but even today the special foods and traditional religious celebrations the Minorcans brought with them remain a colorful part of the city's heritage.

GATORIN' TAILS & TALES

DR. CHARLIE RENTZ

ACKNOWLEDGMENTS

There are so many people to acknowledge and thank for making this book possible.

To my incredible wife, Marcia, thank you for loving me and for being my soulmate. I am still surprised you stayed with me after taking you gatorin' on our third date. Thank you for reading and editing the manuscript (several times) and offering suggestions. Thank you for your many years of supporting me being an alligator trapper. You are great at gatorin' yourself!

To my sister-in-law, Shelli, for editing the manuscript. You have spent countless hours fine-tuning my grammar and syntax to make sense to a reader who is not familiar with gatorin'. Thank you for making the trip from Texas to Florida to accompany me on running permits and getting first-hand experience in doing a live capture of an eight-foot alligator.

To Story Sanctum, my wonderful publisher. Shawn and Jen, you two are the best! This final stage of the book would not have come together without your expertise, final editing, creativity, cover design, and wisdom. You made this process a privilege, and a pleasure. I look forward to working with you again on my next book.

To Elizabeth Sims for your inspiration. Back in 2019, you

gave me a copy of your book, "You've Got A Book In You." It took me a while.

To my many friends, nuisance alligator trappers, and agents who have hunted/trapped with me and covered permits with and for me. Olin, Scott, Lonnie, James, Fat Truck Driver, Lee, David, Travis, Kevin, Robert, Mike F., Brandon, Jimmy, Cameron, Phillip. Thanks to Mickey F. for his help and coaching when I first became a nuisance alligator trapper. And thanks to everyone on the SNAP team.

To my four sons, Caleb, Cody, Keyton, and Josh. Thank you for accompanying me and helping me capture many, many alligators. I awakened you in the middle of the night to assist me on eCalls on numerous occasions, and I called on you to help me drag very large alligators to the trailer. You guys are now the 8th generation of alligator hunters in our family.

Although you are no longer with us in this life, I am thankful for my mother, Dolores, and my grandfather (Gerald) Pappy, who taught me gatorin' and repeated the stories over and over to me of my Minorcan heritage and my alligator-trapping heritage until those stories were forever ingrained in my soul. I now share some of those stories in this book. From your stories, I came to know my great-grandfathers: Robert, Joseph, Jose Vitorio, and Gaspar.

Most of all, I am thankful to God for giving me an incredible heritage, a wonderful family, and amazing friends. I thank

God for allowing me to carry on this "family tradition," for keeping me safe, and for allowing me to write this book and share some of these stories along with my own story as it pertains to alligators.

ABOUT THE AUTHOR

Dr. Charles D. ("Charlie") Rentz is a sixth-generation native Floridian who retired in 2024 after serving for nearly four decades as a pastor in the Florida Conference of the United Methodist Church. A graduate of Florida Southern College and Emory University, he earned his doctorate from Boston University.

Charlie and his wife, Dr. Marcia Rentz, share a blended family of five grown children—and a lively household that includes two Labrador retrievers, a rescued/rehabbed squirrel, and a rescued/rehabbed turtle. When they're not visiting family, Charlie and Marcia can be found lobstering in the Florida Keys, mountain biking, camping, or practicing archery on 3D courses.

Never one to sit still for long, Charlie continues to serve as a licensed nuisance alligator trapper for Manatee County, spending much of his week out "gatorin'" in the Florida wilds he's called home his entire life.

www.ingramcontent.com/pod-product-compliance
Lightning Source LLC
Chambersburg PA
CBHW020938090426
42736CB00010B/1181